Beyond the Blueprint

Directions for Research on Head Start's Families

Deborah A. Phillips and Natasha J. Cabrera, Editors

Roundtable on Head Start Research

Board on Children, Youth, and Families

Commission on Behavioral and Social Sciences and Education
National Research Council

Institute of Medicine

National Academy Press
Washington, D.C. 1996

National Academy Press • 2101 Constitution Avenue, N.W. • Washington, D.C. 20418

NOTICE: The project that is the subject of this report was approved by the Governing Board of the National Research Council, whose members are drawn from the councils of the National Academy of Sciences, the National Academy of Engineering, and the Institute of Medicine. The members of the committee responsible for the report were chosen for their special competences and with regard for appropriate balance.

This report has been reviewed by a group other than the authors according to procedures approved by a Report Review Committee consisting of members of the National Academy of Sciences, the National Academy of Engineering, and the Institute of Medicine.

Support for this project was provided by the Administration for Children and Families of the U.S. Department of Health and Human Services and the Ford Foundation.

ROUNDTABLE ON HEAD START RESEARCH

SHELDON H. WHITE (*Chair*), Department of Psychology, Harvard
University
DUANE ALEXANDER, National Institute of Child Health and
Human Development, National Institutes of Health
W. STEVEN BARNETT, Graduate School of Education, Rutgers
University
DONNA BRYANT, Frank Porter Graham Development Center,
University of North Carolina, Chapel Hill
CAROLE CLARKE, Center for Education and Manpower Resources,
Ukiah, California
THOMAS COOK, Center for Urban Affairs, Northwestern University
CLAUDIA COULTON, Center for Urban Poverty and Social Change,
Mandel School of Applied Social Sciences, Case Western Reserve
University
WILLIE EPPS, Southern Illinois University, Edwardsville
LINDA ESPINOSA, Bright Horizons, Cambridge, Massachusetts
EUGENE GARCIA, Graduate School of Education, University of
California, Berkeley
CLAUDE GOLDENBERG, Department of Teacher Education,
California State University, Long Beach
NOREEN GOLDMAN, Woodrow Wilson School of Public and
International Affairs, Princeton University
FERNANDO GUERRA, San Antonio Metropolitan Health District,
San Antonio, Texas
JANE KNITZER, National Center for Children in Poverty, New York
City
RONALD LALLY, Center for Child and Family Studies, Far West
Laboratory, Sausalito, California
ELEANOR MACCOBY, Department of Psychology, Stanford
University
MARTHA MOOREHOUSE, U.S. Department of Health and Human
Services, Washington, D.C.
GREGG POWELL, National Head Start Association, Alexandria,
Virginia
SUZANNE RANDOLPH, Department of Family Studies, University of
Maryland
JACK P. SHONKOFF, Heller Graduate School, Brandeis University

Contents

The National Academy of Sciences is a private, nonprofit, self-perpetuating society of distinguished scholars engaged in scientific and engineering research, dedicated to the furtherance of science and technology and to their use for the general welfare. Upon the authority of the charter granted to it by the Congress in 1863, the Academy has a mandate that requires it to advise the federal government on scientific and technical matters. Dr. Bruce M. Alberts is president of the National Academy of Sciences.

The National Academy of Engineering was established in 1964, under the charter of the National Academy of Sciences, as a parallel organization of outstanding engineers. It is autonomous in its administration and in the selection of its members, sharing with the National Academy of Sciences the responsibility for advising the federal government. The National Academy of Engineering also sponsors engineering programs aimed at meeting national needs, encourages education and research, and recognizes the superior achievements of engineers. Dr. Harold Liebowitz is president of the National Academy of Engineering.

The Institute of Medicine was established in 1970 by the National Academy of Sciences to secure the services of eminent members of appropriate professions in the examination of policy matters pertaining to the health of the public. The Institute acts under the responsibility given to the National Academy of Sciences by its congressional charter to be an adviser to the federal government and, upon its own initiative, to identify issues of medical care, research, and education. Dr. Kenneth I. Shine is president of the Institute of Medicine.

The National Research Council was organized by the National Academy of Sciences in 1916 to associate the broad community of science and technology with the Academy's purposes of furthering knowledge and advising the federal government. Functioning in accordance with general policies determined by the Academy, the Council has become the principal operating agency of both the National Academy of Sciences and the National Academy of Engineering in providing services to the government, the public, and the scientific and engineering communities. The Council is administered jointly by both Academies and the Institute of Medicine. Dr. Bruce M. Alberts and Dr. Harold Liebowitz are chairman and vice chairman, respectively, of the National Research Council.

Preface

Head Start is a comprehensive program serving poor children and their families in several thousand localities in the United States. The program is well known. Public acceptance of it is high. Yet public understanding of what Head Start is and does remains shallow. For many, understanding of the program's accomplishments has been built on intermittent discussions of the findings of a thin thread of controversial evaluation research. But studies of Head Start to date have been limited in quantity and scope. The Advisory Committee on Head Start Quality and Expansion, reviewing the program's situation in 1993, recommended a long-term research plan for Head Start that places it in the broader context of research on young children, families, and communities, ensures a commitment to ongoing themes, and yet has the flexibility to respond to new and emerging issues (U.S. Department of Health and Human Services, 1993).

The Roundtable on Head Start Research, under the auspices of the National Research Council and the Institute of Medicine, began a series of discussions of new possibilities and new directions for Head Start research with its first meeting in November 1994. The roundtable had two purposes.

First, it sought to find ways to explore more broadly what Head Start has been doing, looking for those aspects of the program that have been understudied. The roundtable also sought new dimensions for Head Start research made possible by recent work in the behavioral and social sciences, notably broader disciplinary participation in research on children and families, a growing knowledge base regarding community and family processes, and increased reliance on research designs that use a plurality of methods, including those that are sensitive to and appropriate for local contexts. The roundtable gave special attention to the question of Head Start's effects on poor families. Much testimony and many informal observations say that such effects have been substantial, yet they have been little studied in the past. From a scientific point of view, we are today in a better position to study them than we ever have been before.

Second, the roundtable sought to find avenues of research that would help Head Start to recognize and deal with historically new contingencies. The problems of poverty have changed during Head Start's 30 years. The lives of the poor have become more difficult, carried on in the midst of a new climate of violence. Statistics say that the number of single parents has been increasing dramatically. Behind the statistics, quietly, many poor people have been moving away from the one-household, one-family configuration that was fairly standard 30 years ago. Head Start's children are a more mixed group. About 20 percent of them speak a language other than English. Most Head Start centers are now bicultural; a good number are multicultural. Head Start centers must operate differently. They serve the educational, health, and familial well-being of their children, now as always. But centers work in a surround of schools, health care organizations, and social service programs that are constantly changing.

When Head Start was created in 1965, there was a movement toward scientific management of domestic programs. One of the hopes of that era was that large-scale, "summative" studies of programs such as Head Start could use one or two psychometric indicators and simply and univocally determine whether or not the program was working. The evaluation research of that first generation regularly demonstrated that Head Start graduates showed positive improvements on school readiness tests, achievement tests, and other tests of cognitive skills. Follow-up studies showed that the test score gains faded out by the time the children reached the third grade. In effect, the control children who did not participate in Head Start caught up to the levels of performance of the Head Start participants. A few contended that such fadeouts showed that the initial gains of the children were not quite real. What is conspicuous in this legacy of research is the limited instrumentation used to assess outcomes in comparison with the broad goals that parents, Congress, and administrators have assigned to Head Start.

It is unreasonable to expect that one year of a Head Start preschool experience should prove itself by producing benefits indefinitely into the future. There have been studies showing that some preschool programs for poor children—generally better funded than Head Start—have produced detectable positive benefits for their children extending into adulthood, despite the appearance of early fadeout. The findings of such studies are currently being pursued. It is not easy to follow children in longitudinal investigations lasting 12-15 years; such studies are rare and difficult. But the question of what happens to Head Start children at age 4 cannot be completely delegated to exotic studies of dropout rates, delinquency, and drugs in the high school years. We need to look more carefully at the experiences of Head Start children and their families in the preschool years, as well as the near-term consequences of those experiences as the child enters the school years.

Beginning in 1988, the Administration for Children, Youth, and Families (ACYF) initiated a series of planning efforts to consider desirable strategies for Head Start research and evaluation. A first ACYF committee (1990), often referred to as the Blueprint Committee, opened the door to a new order of Head Start studies. In its report, *Head Start Research and Evaluation: A Blueprint for the Future*, the committee took the essential step of recognizing the fundamental pluralism of Head Start's activities and research needs (U.S. Department of Health and Human Services, 1990):

- Head Start centers are located in different parts of the country. They serve children of diverse minority groups and children with special needs—handicapped children, migrant children, children of immigrants. Head Start centers differ one from another in important respects because they have to be different. Research addressed to a Head Start center has to consider its population, its methods, and its goals.

- Head Start centers are not purely and simply preschools. They have responsibilities for providing their children with a positive preschool experience, for work with families, for nutrition, for health screening and referral, and for community action. Studies of whether and how a Head Start center is working have to examine this spectrum of activities.

- Since Head Start is a pluralistic, decentralized program, individuals at a number of levels have significant responsibilities for steering and guiding Head Start efforts, and new knowledge could and should benefit their work. Those with a legitimate interest in Head Start research include

Head Start center directors, families, and people with responsibilities for Head Start's special populations and activities. This is not to say that a proper piece of research on Head Start should say something useful and interesting to everybody. It is to say that people involved with Head Start look at it through different perspectives. There are valid, meaningful, and practically useful questions about Head Start that can be framed from perspectives other than a top-down one.

The work of the Roundtable on Head Start Research, discussed in this report, represents an effort to set forward new possibilities for research that can shed light on important but underexplored aspects of Head Start, in the spirit of the Blueprint Committee's report. Members of the roundtable are a distinguished group of individuals drawn from government, universities, medicine, Head Start organizations, family support programs, and private foundations. Collectively, they bring many years of experience with Head Start, research, government, and program management to the table. Discussions at the roundtable's meetings were lively, thoughtful, and deeply searching. The roundtable addressed itself to a series of questions about Head Start as a program, about the circumstances of the poor, and about state-of-the-art behavioral and social science research. Among the issues discussed were the following:

• *The Need to Study Family Dynamics and Development.* We often talk about poor children's families as though they exist in two or three static configurations. But children's family circumstances often change as they grow up. Furthermore, there are indications that more complex kinds of household arrangements are emerging among the poor. How should one think about Head Start's work with families and its effects in more complex and adequate terms?

• *New Possibilities for Studying Social and Emotional Development.* When Head Start began, a renaissance of developmental psychology was under way, organized around the remarkable studies of children's cognitive development of the Swiss biologist, Jean Piaget. Early discussions of the possibilities of Head Start tended to center on cognitive development as an issue and a goal—although periodic surveys of Head Start center directors indicated that they regarded the social and emotional development of their children as a more important short-term goal. Today, there are many new research approaches and theoretical ideas addressed to children's social and emotional development. Can we use this new work to explore in a more complete way what happens to a child during and after a Head Start experience?

• *Harvesting Local Programmatic Inventions.* We know that Head Start as a decentralized pluralistic program exists on the basis of many local programmatic inventions and adaptations. Can we use research to explore and harvest the products of some Head Start centers for the benefit of others—elsewhere in Head Start, in the schools, in day care centers—interested in preschool programs for poor children? Such research would fulfill the hopes of those who, in the early years of Head Start, predicted that it might become a national laboratory of early childhood education.

• *Mental Health Issues in Head Start.* The experience of the poor now includes periodic exposures to unpredictable violence. And poor children and members of their families now show emotional reactions to such experiences of a kind that, in adults, would be characterized as symptomatic of post-traumatic stress disorders. Can we use research to find ways to help children, families, and Head Start staff deal with such experiences?

These issues are a few among the large number of questions and possibilities discussed by the Roundtable on Head Start Research and reflected in this report. Our goal was not to engage in the preparation of a research program or priorities for Head Start, nor was it to engage in detailed research planning. We sought to open doors and to increase understanding of what Head Start is doing, what it is and is not accomplishing. The report to follow gives an excellent sense of what we found.

Sheldon H. White, Chair
Roundtable on Head Start Research

Acknowledgments

This report represents the collaborative efforts of many individuals, particularly the roundtable members and staff whose names appear at the beginning of the document. All sections of the report benefited tremendously from the insightful remarks provided by the invited speakers at the workshops convened by the roundtable; speakers are listed in Appendix B. The committee expresses its deep appreciation to them.

The leadership and contributions of Natasha Cabrera, director of the roundtable, in particular, were essential at every stage of the process, from the initial formulation of the report through its final preparation. The contributions of other members of the staff were also significant. As director of the Board on Children, Youth, and Families, Deborah Phillips provided invaluable guidance and support to the roundtable. Karen Autrey, project assistant to the roundtable, worked especially hard on this project and on the report. Her special contributions and dedication to the roundtable are gratefully acknowledged. The roundtable also acknowledges the substantial contributions of editor Christine McShane and of Anne Bridgman, communications officer of the Board on Children, Youth, and Families; they improved the appearance and accuracy of the final product immeasurably.

This report was funded by the Administration on Children, Youth, and Families of the U.S. Department of Health and Human Services. This agency's willingness to finance a roundtable that was charged with envisioning new directions for Head Start research took no small degree of courage and commitment. The encouragement and funding provided by the leadership and staff of ACYF are gratefully acknowledged.

Sheldon H. White, Chair
Roundtable on Head Start Research

Beyond the Blueprint

Directions for Research on Head Start's Families

1

Introduction

On its 30th anniversary, Head Start has much to celebrate. It also has to confront many social and economic challenges that have emerged since its 1965 inception. The lives of families and children who live in poverty today are more complicated and precarious than in the recent past (Houston, McLoyd, and Garcia Coll, 1994). Violence and substance abuse, periods of homelessness, and serious mental illness are increasingly commonplace among the families that Head Start serves. Accordingly, many perceive that the share of eligible children with serious behavioral problems and special needs is on the rise. Today's poor families are also likely to have complex and shifting family structures, highly diverse ethnic and linguistic backgrounds, and uneven education and employment histories. Many also display remarkable strength and courage as they struggle to provide for their children in less than hospitable communities.

At the same time, the prevailing expectations of these families, many of which are headed by single-mothers, now include training, education, and work. These new problems and expectations for families living in poverty are complicating the task of providing high-quality services to them. Fortunately, we have learned a great deal about the needs of young children and the attributes of services and supports that can assist families living under extremely stressful circumstances.

ESTABLISHMENT OF THE ROUNDTABLE ON
HEAD START RESEARCH

This is the context in which the Roundtable on Head Start Research considered directions for research that will generate a broader understanding of what is happening to families *in* Head Start and *because of* Head Start. The roundtable was established in September 1994 with support from the Administration on Children, Youth, and Families (ACYF). It will complete its work by August 1996, meeting nine times during its two-year lifespan.

The purpose of the roundtable is to provide a systematic analysis of research needs relevant to the changing context that Head Start faces as it moves into its fourth decade. It is best understood in the context of two prior reports (see Appendix A). The report of the Advisory Panel for the Head Start Evaluation Design Project, *Head Start Research and Evaluation: A Blueprint for the Future* (U.S. Department of Health and Human Services, 1990), defined a set of guiding principles for the selection and conduct of future Head Start research and evaluation efforts. These principles emphasized, in particular, that the highest priority for research by or for Head Start should be given to those investigations that hold greatest promise of providing knowledge about "which Head Start practices maximize benefits for children and families with different characteristics under what types of circumstances" (p. 3), and about how best to sustain these benefits. The *Blueprint* report also recommended an overall research strategy that recognizes the diversity of Head Start programs rather than a single large-scale study.

The *Blueprint* recommendations were carried forward into the report of the Advisory Committee on Head Start Quality and Expansion, *Creating a 21st Century Head Start* (U.S. Department of Health and Human Services, 1993). This report specifically identified the need to reinvigorate the role of Head Start as a national laboratory for best practices in early childhood and family support services during this period of program reexamination, improvement, and expansion. The roundtable is part of ACYF's efforts to fulfill this goal.

The roundtable's broad charge, as articulated by Olivia Golden, ACYF's commissioner, is to inform the agency's efforts to develop short- and long-term research agendas that move the general set of principles recommended by the *Blueprint* report (see Appendix A) to more specific directions for the future. She asked that the roundtable consider research that does justice to the richness of Head Start, applies the *Blueprint* principles to specific cases, links to developments in the broader fields of early childhood and child development research, considers opportunities for partnerships with programs, and helps ACYF to identify significant questions for the next generation of Head Start research. The roundtable members were not asked to establish priorities among generated research questions or to develop a complete research agenda.

More specifically, the roundtable's charge was to focus on the implications of the changing family, community, and policy contexts within which Head Start now operates for future research on the children and families it serves, with an emphasis on preschool-age children. Great importance was attached to investigations that can contribute significantly to increasing the quality and effectiveness of the program in furthering children's development.

By request, the first three meetings of the roundtable were guided by ACYF's conviction that research to date on Head Start has not given adequate attention to one of the most distinctive and potentially powerful components of the program—family involvement and its effects on a wide range of developmental outcomes. Family outcomes were portrayed by ACYF as the untold story of Head Start, the source of many of the economic benefits of Head Start, and perhaps the explanatory link to its benefits for children. The agency was also interested in obtaining input into its new Descriptive Study of Families served by Head Start, the goal of which is to document families' trajectory into and beyond Head Start.

In response to ACYF's interests, the roundtable's initial deliberations considered research that takes Head Start families as the unit of analysis and explicitly addressed research on Head Start in the context of family and community life. Its discussions, nevertheless, turned frequently toward issues regarding the quality of Head Start's developmental program— its curriculum, its staff, its direct services for children, and child outcomes. Several of the roundtable members felt that, although Head Start's family-level services and effects are critical and have been neglected in research, many of the basic issues for children also require concerted attention as Head Start enters a period in which its children may actually experience less parental time (due to employment and economic demands) and may— in some states—face diminished services in other sectors. As a result, some child-level research questions are integrated into the broad framework of this report, which was primarily shaped by the charge to consider research on Head Start's families. This is particularly evident in Chapter 3, which addresses research on the growing ethnic and linguistic diversity of the Head Start population.

In subsequent meetings, the roundtable considered innovative efforts to assess preschool child outcomes, addressed ways of ensuring that investments in Head Start research reap greater payoffs through archiving and secondary analytic work, convened pertinent agencies and research teams to discuss critical elements of an integrated early childhood research agenda, and provided a forum for Head Start practitioners to identify their field-based research needs and interests.

The impetus for creating the roundtable has several sources:

• Head Start has been chronically underserved by research, with episodes of low activity followed by periods of high activity. Of a $3.5 billion Head Start budget in 1995, about $23 million (approximately 0.6 percent) is allocated to research.

• The research on Head Start and other early intervention programs that has most influenced public discussion is now outdated and limited. For example, for various historical and practical reasons, IQ and school achievement tests dominated the early evaluations of Head Start. The diverse accomplishments of this complex, locally tailored program with several distinct objectives have been underexplored and thus constitute an untold story.

• The Report of the Advisory Committee on Head Start Quality and Expansion, *Creating a 21st Century Head Start* (U.S. Department of Health and Human Services, 1993), specifically identified the need to reinvigorate the role of Head Start as a national laboratory for best practices in early childhood and family support services during this period of program reexamination, improvement, and expansion. Given a decentralized program, efforts to track program activities, let alone to redirect and improve them, require a strong and enduring infrastructure for Head Start research. An important step in this direction involves identifying the obstacles to establishing a national laboratory.

THE ROUNDTABLE'S DELIBERATIONS ON FAMILY-LEVEL RESEARCH

The departure point, then, for the roundtable's discussion of future research on Head Start families involved assessing, through a series of three one-day workshops, what is known about the demographics, life circumstances and needs of the eligible population and about efforts—within and beyond Head Start—to address these needs. The diversity of the Head

Start population and its implications for the program, and hence for research, were also explicitly addressed. Box 1 summarizes several basic facts about Head Start programs and their clients.

The discussions of the contemporary portrait of life in poverty that emerged from the workshops raised critical issues regarding the priorities that should guide the future development of Head Start programs. On one hand, Head Start was *not* designed primarily to meet the child care needs of full-time, full-year employed parents. Nor was it conceived to address problems of community violence, provide literacy and job training for parents, or ensure that the full complement of health services is provided to young children. On the other hand, Head Start's comprehensive mandate to improve the life chances of children living in poverty takes on new meaning as the composition of the poverty population and the conditions of these children's lives undergo dramatic changes. For example, how do Head Start staff attempt to engage children whose lives are constantly disrupted by violence in their neighborhoods? Such issues raise basic challenges to the original conception of Head Start.

The roundtable members, though keenly aware of these tensions, did not attempt to redefine the goals that guide the scope of services that Head Start offers poor children and their families. They did, however, recognize that, because the face of poverty has changed, some adaptations are likely to be required if Head Start is to produce the outcomes for children for which it was designed. They sought to identify a finite set of issues for research that reflect the changing context of Head Start and, as such, have not received the research attention within Head Start that they warrant. Recognizing that Head Start is likely to face some difficult trade-offs in the years ahead, the roundtable members aimed to ensure that relevant data are available for future deliberations concerning the goals and scope of this long-standing, national intervention program. They sought specifically to move beyond general strategies and principles for research to specific, contemporary issues that warrant empirical attention. What next steps for research offer fruitful starting points for productive research sequences?

SCOPE OF THE REPORT

This report summarizes the deliberations of the first three roundtable meetings regarding research on Head Start families.

Taking the *Blueprint* principles as its point of departure for developing

Box 1
Facts About Head Start

Head Start, first enacted as part of the Johnson administration's War on Poverty, is an early childhood program for low-income children that was recently reauthorized through fiscal 1998. Head Start is administered by ACYF of the Department of Health and Human Services. This antipoverty program funds community-based agencies to provide services in five component areas: education, physical and mental health, social services, nutrition, and parent involvement. As of fiscal 1993:

• To be eligible for Head Start a child must be living in a family whose income is below the federal poverty line, currently $14,350 for a family of four. Ten percent of Head Start children came from families whose income is higher than the poverty line;

• Head Start programs are comprised of both center-based programs and home-based programs. There are about 2,000 Head Start programs currently in operation around the country; 612 Head Start programs include a home-based program. Home-based services were provided to 49,442 children by 4,415 home visitors;

• A total of 713,903 children were enrolled and, of that total, 33,886 children were enrolled in Head Start's migrant programs. Since 1965, 13,854,000 children have been served;

• Overall, 24 percent of enrolled children were Hispanic, 36 percent were African American, 4 percent were Native American, 3 percent were Asian, and 33 percent were white. And 13.2 percent of the enrolled children had disabilities;

• In all, 3 percent of children served in Head Start were 3 years of age or younger. Infants and toddlers were served under two programs, the Parent and Child Center program (PCC) and the migrant program. There are no specific regulations governing Head Start programs for infants and toddlers;

• There were 129,800 paid staff and 1,157,000 volunteers; 81 percent have degrees in early childhood education or have obtained the Child Development Associate (CDA) credential;

• The average salary for a Head Start teacher was $15,000 and for an aide was $9,500; and

• Almost 33 percent of the Head Start staff were parents of current or former Head Start children. Over 706,000 parents volunteered in their local Head Start program.

a more specific set of possibilities for research on Head Start's families, the report first outlines general themes that emerged from the workshops and that provided a conceptual framework for approaching Head Start families from a research perspective (Chapter 2). Chapters 3 through 5 focus on specific issues that emerged as central topics during the workshops and the roundtable's subsequent deliberations. They represent issues that have surfaced in recent years, as a result of changing demographic and social conditions of low-income families and, as such, have not been adequately explored by research:

- The challenges posed to Head Start by the increasing ethnic and linguistic diversity of the families it serves (Chapter 3);
- The need to embed research on Head Start within its community context, paying specific attention to the effects on Head Start and its families of violent environments (Chapter 4); and
- The implications of the changing economic landscape and the structure of income support policies for the poor for how Head Start works with families, and what it means to offer families a high-quality program (Chapter 5).

Each of these issue-oriented chapters provides a brief synopsis of the topic, followed by a discussion of the researchable issues addressed by the roundtable members and suggestions for next steps for Head Start research. The next steps for research represent several topics that merit specific research attention because they have been neglected by past efforts, they are emerging as important social factors affecting the program itself, and they have important consequences for research on family-level effects and how to sustain them.

The roundtable members distinguished three types of research agendas: (1) a descriptive agenda focused on understanding *who* is served by Head Start and *what* Head Start programs do in their day-to-day interaction with children and families, (2) an agenda aimed at identifying ways in which Head Start can mount high-quality programs for today's children and families in today's communities, and (3) an outcome agenda that addresses the questions "Does it work?" "For whom does it work best?" and "What are we getting for the investment?" This classification scheme guides the organization of the suggested next steps for research, which are presented in each chapter and summarized in Table 1.

These agendas are, of course, interdependent. The question "Does it

TABLE 1 Summary of Next Steps for Research

| | TYPE OF AGENDA | | |
Proposed Research	Descriptive	Quality	Outcome
Chapter 3: **Recognizing Diversity**			
(3-1) Classroom language mix, instructional practices and child development	X	X	X
(3-2) Home-Head Start interactions in the context of diversity	X	X	X
(3-3) Participation in Head Start: Role of language, migrant and immigrant status	X	X	X
(3-4) Family support and linguistic diversity		X	X
(3-5) Program adjustments to shifting demographics	X	X	
Chapter 4: **Community-Head Start Linkages**			
(4-1) Family-level effects: parents' capacity to mobilize community resources	X	X	X
(4-2) Impact of community-level resources on Head Start	X		X
(4-3) Community-level effects of Head Start	X	X	X
(4-4) Exposure to community and domestic violence	X		
(4-5) Staff and parent views of the effects of violence	X		
(4-6) Head Start's role in violence prevention	X		X

TABLE 1 Continued

Proposed Research	TYPE OF AGENDA		
	Descriptive	Quality	Outcome
Chapter 5: **Families in a Changing Economic Landscape**			
(5-1) Income sources of Head Start families	X		
(5-2) Head Start's effect on parents' employment and earnings trajectories	X		
(5-3) Literacy and job training	X	X	X
(5-4) Parent involvement practices	X	X	X
(5-5) Cost-effective approaches to providing full-time, full-year care	X	X	X

Note: The numbers in the table correspond to the sections in Chapters 3, 4, and 5 that list next steps for research.

work?" will be most usefully answered by research that examines where Head Start is working well, for whom, and why; where it fails; and how to make it better. The next steps for research suggested by roundtable members encompass each of these types of research and often blend several of them. Some of the issues that were discussed are so new to Head Start that purely descriptive research is a logical first step (e.g., research on community and domestic violence, and on the income sources of Head Start families). Others are more amenable to research designs that emphasize issues of quality and effectiveness (e.g., research on the role of family support staff with linguistically and ethnically diverse families). Table 1 provides a summary of suggested next steps for research organized by the three types of research agendas.

It is important to emphasize that, although the roundtable members focused mainly on "what to study" rather than on "how to study it," they acknowledged the difficulties of conducting research on Head Start that produces valid estimates of program effects. This difficulty arises from several sources: (1) it is difficult and costly to implement randomized trials and other designs known to produce unbiased estimates of Head Start programs (e.g., experimentally intervening in Head Start programs to create quality differences), (2) there is no broad consensus regarding the parameters of an appropriate control group for a study of Head Start's effects, and (3) there is an inadequate research base with which to judge the validity of estimates of Head Start produced by other methodological approaches (e.g., comparing groups that are different using statistical controls for observable differences).

A fundamental concern that conditioned and influenced all the roundtable deliberations was the possibility that federal and private funding for Head Start research may become increasingly scarce. In this context, it becomes imperative for the agency to have in place an infrastructure that creates and maintains a research agenda that is collaborative, is focused, and can produce the knowledge needed for improving the effectiveness of Head Start. The roundtable, recognizing that ACYF not only funds research in Head Start but is also the agency whose future can be most affected by this research, also touched on the importance of broadening responsibility for Head Start research to include research agencies and private foundations. Indeed, the membership of the roundtable includes representation from these sectors in part to signify the range of institutions that are suited to contribute to the future of research on Head Start.

The roundtable's initial discussion of infrastructure issues is reflected in Chapter 6, which acknowledges that programmatic local innovation merits research attention in order to import its successful experiences to other programs. In this context, the synergy between researchers and program staff is critical and highlights a fundamental need to build a research infrastructure for Head Start. Along these lines, this report summarizes the roundtable's discussions of the role of research in documenting and extending the lessons gained from programs that have adopted particularly innovative approaches to addressing the needs of today's families in poverty.

It is important to emphasize that the report touches only lightly on Head Start's educational program, peer relations and social skills, child outcomes, sibling effects, health, and other dimensions of its child-focused goals. This should not be construed as reflecting any lack of concern on behalf of the roundtable about these issues. Rather, it reflects ACYF's specific charge to the roundtable to focus on research that takes as its primary concern Head Start families and family-level effects insofar as they mediate effects on children in the short and longer term. Consequently, the research agenda on Head Start's families outlined in this report is not to be regarded as a frame for the entirety of Head Start research. There are still many issues about the content of the program and effects on children's learning and development that need to be resolved.

Each of the topics addressed in this report generated lively discussion that included divergent points of view about the most appropriate next steps for research. This report does not offer consensus recommendations for research directons on Head Start's families. Rather, it points to several promising next steps for research that hold the potential to reinvigorate Head Start's role as a national laboratory, link research on Head Start to other exciting developments in allied fields of research, and ensure that research on Head Start is immediately relevant to the program's efforts to provide high-quality, effective services.

2

Studying Head Start's Families:
General Themes

This chapter highlights several of the general themes that emerged from the roundtable discussions. The roundtable members, throughout their deliberations, sought to establish a useful framework within which a progression of studies on Head Start children and families could be developed. They considered approaches to reconceptualizing traditional notions of parental involvement and family support in order to capture more dynamic views of the family–Head Start interface. Their objective was to offer a guide to research that: (1) provides an accurate portrait of families' experiences in Head Start, (2) identifies effective approaches to working with families, and (3) documents the benefits to families and their children of the nation's investment in Head Start.

The wealth of background information to which roundtable members were exposed (see Chapters 3 through 5) led them to emphasize that:

• The relationship between Head Start and its families is reciprocal—Head Start both affects and responds to families; mutual adaptation between families and programs is the process of interest;

• The family–Head Start relationship takes many forms and evolves over time; it is best approached as a process, rather than as a discrete set of activities that operate as inputs to parent and child outcomes;

• Although the primary caretaker at home is the pivotal connection to the family, the consequences of any family's encounter with Head Start extend beyond those who are directly involved, to other members of the family and the kinship and fictive kin networks in which many Head Start families are embedded.

Approaching research on Head Start families within a framework that emphasizes mutual adaptation, change over time, and effects beyond the immediate parent-child dyad has implications for virtually every aspect of research that is discussed in the succeeding chapters of this report.

> *Suzanne Randolph called for more descriptive case studies of the complexities of families' circumstances. Poor families tend to organize themselves into multigenerational units and many bridge traditional and nontraditional norms within their own culture in rearing their children. We need to understand how such multigenerational families interact with and are influenced by Head Start centers.*

- *It is important to revisit how the family is construed in Head Start research and who is considered to be the client.*

Traditional descriptive categorizations of families (e.g., single- and two-parent; white, black, and Hispanic) fail to capture the aspects of family structure and functioning that may account for most of the variance in how families relate to and are affected by Head Start, and in turn mediate Head Start's effects on their children. In particular, definitions of family need to be more descriptive of the relationships, dimensions of culture and ethnicity, and economic circumstances that affect children's lives (e.g., Randolph, 1995). A family's multigenerational configuration and its implications for how childrearing responsibilities are allocated may, for example, provide a better guide for selecting who Head Start should attempt to involve than traditional approaches that assume the mother is the sole or principal caregiver. In other cases, the immigrant status of families may be a better indicator of a family's needs and interests than their ethnicity. Many of these important family features, including family configuration, fluctuate over time, adding to the instability that itself may affect Head Start's capacity to foster children's development and helpful relationships with their families.

An effort aimed at providing descriptive information on children and

---

Box 2

The Head Start Family Information System is a self-report instrument being developed to obtain on-line baseline information from programs on Head Start families and children at the time of enrollment. Its five modules address: (1) family and child background information, (2) education, including literacy, (3) health and nutrition, (4) social services, and (5) parent involvement.

---

families is the Head Start Family Information System, now under development (see Box 2). It offers a first attempt by ACYF to generate a profile of Head Start families, and, as such, offers a focal point for efforts to ensure the collection of data that capture the most meaningful dimensions of family structure and family life.

• *Documentation of the process of selection into Head Start is critical for tailoring programs to the needs of the communities they serve, for outreach to underserved families, and for interpreting program effects.*

The families who participate in Head Start are not randomly selected from among the poverty population (Hofferth, 1994). This raises important questions about who does not get into Head Start and why, particularly in light of growing concerns that this relatively high-quality but part-day program may be inaccessible to single parents who are struggling to combine childrearing and work. It is, therefore, important to ascertain the quality and stability of the care that eligible children are getting in the absence of Head Start.

In view of these concerns, the roundtable members stressed the need for more complete and authoritative epidemiological data regarding children who do and do not enter Head Start. For Head Start clients, we need to know about level, amount, and kinds of participation. For nonparticipants, we need to know what types of early childhood programs are available to them and their usage of other resources.

An important epidemiological effort that aims to gain a greater understanding of the trajectories of social and emotional development in young children is the National Institute of Mental Health's (NIMH) multisite, longitudinal study titled Use, Need, Outcomes, and Costs for Child and Adolescent Populations (UNOCCAP). To determine the influence of Head Start participation on children's development, ACYF is collaborating with NIMH on a supplemental sample of Head Start programs and families. The NIMH project was initiated to explore the need for and use of mental health services among children and adolescents and the influence of family, cultural, community, and service system factors on service needs, utilization, and outcomes. ACYF's participation in this project will enable a more in-depth examination of issues related to four-year-olds in general and Head Start children and families in particular. Among the research questions that the UNOCCAP project is addressing are: How do children enrolled in Head Start compare with a community sample of children in terms of key social and emotional characteristics? How do Head Start children's mental health needs compare with those of other, non-Head Start children?

Sandra Hofferth's research on Head Start families has revealed that working single-parent families, as well as Hispanics, are underrepresented. All Head Start families are very disadvantaged economically, even within the poverty population.

• *Efforts to describe how Head Start relates to and involves family members, and to identify successful strategies for involving them, need to capture families' natural progressions into, through, and beyond Head Start.*

Numerous presentations made to the roundtable emphasized that parent involvement is inadequately captured by research designs that adopt a one-time approach to classifying a program's parent involvement strategies (e.g., classroom volunteer, bus driver, roles in governance, participation in home visits and literacy classes) and then compare programs in terms of whether and how much they affect family outcomes. The challenge, instead, is to describe and study the consequences of the *process* of a family's engagement with Head Start from selection through varying forms and intensities of participation to post-graduation.

This involves understanding the pathways that family members follow given different starting points, differing goals and strategies for their participation in Head Start (e.g., improve parenting skills, prepare for employment, develop "executive" skills as advocates for their children), and different post-graduation circumstances. An important element of research on the process of family engagement involves investigating the factors that enable parents to transfer the skills learned during their involvement with Head Start to their lives after Head Start. For example, how does a family's involvement with Head Start affect their involvement with their child's elementary school? It is also critical to recognize that some changes, especially those that take place after a family is no longer involved with Head Start, may not be measurable within the one- or two-year time frame of most evaluations and may be best captured in longitudinal research.

> *Efforts aimed at discerning parents' progress as a consequence of their involvement in Head Start may entail identifying parents who have or have not made major changes in their lives, Marlys Gustafson noted.*

An important aspect of the trajectory into and beyond Head Start is children's transition from Head Start to public school. In order to assess the effectiveness of providing comprehensive, continuous, and coordinated services to Head Start families and children from the time of Head Start enrollment to kindergarten through the third grade of public school, ACYF has initiated the Evaluation of Head Start/Public School Early Childhood Transition Demonstration projects. The Transition Projects are designed to document the progress of children and families enrolled in Head Start as they make the transition from Head Start to elementary school up to third grade. The evaluation will provide data regarding the effectiveness of the Transition Project models in maintaining the gains that children and families achieve while in Head Start, as well as providing information about child, family, school, and service characteristics that may affect this transition process.

> *Heather Weiss and Lynn Kagan argued that most discussions of family effects deal indiscriminantly with "outside" effects— parental employment, family participation in community activities—or "inside" effects—the kinds of person-to-person interchanges that take place within families. We need to look at the ways in which inside and outside variables influence one another.*

- Given that families enter Head Start with vastly different capacities, needs, and orientations toward parent involvement, any effort to assess the effects of their engagement with the program must consider incremental but significant changes, rather than judge all families' accomplishments against preset benchmarks.

Because the consequences of parent involvement are profoundly affected by parents' initial characteristics and circumstances, efforts to understand the efficacy of different processes for engaging parents need to assess individual growth and change from different starting points. For some parents, overcoming disabling levels of depression and being able to get their children dressed and on the bus dependably may be major achievements. For others, progress may be seen in movement from serving as a classroom volunteer to enrollment in community college classes and employment as a teacher. For still others, important accomplishments entail learning to set goals and taking small steps toward achieving those goals—a process that Project Match refers to as the ladder approach (see Box 3).

The fact that most evaluations of government programs cover rela-

---

Box 3

Project Match, described to the roundtable by Toby Herr, is a community-based, welfare-to-work program for residents of a housing development in Chicago that has recently initiated a collaboration with Head Start. This program's decade of experience has taught it that:

- There are multiple routes out of welfare dependence; for some, work prior to education is more effective than the more typical path from education to work;

- There must be a continuum of activities that count as steps on a ladder toward self-sufficiency;

- People should be recognized for achievement of incremental milestones that keep them moving up the ladder; and

- The time frame for leaving welfare dependance must be flexible if success is to be sustained.

Almost half of all parents involved in the project have made steady progress, more than a third unsteady progress (in and out of jobs), and close to a fifth have made no progress at all.

tively short periods of time presents a very serious problem in trying to capture a developmental effect—whether in a child, a family, or a community. Some changes not seen in the normal two-year span of research may quite readily be seen three or four years out. In short, parents' transformation as a consequence of their involvement in Head Start needs to be examined beyond graduation from the program to determine whether Head Start has set in motion longer-lasting changes.

   • *It is important to understand not only the ways in which parents change over the course of their involvement with Head Start, but also the ways in which Head Start adapts to meet the needs of its population.*

Several presentations to the roundtable emphasized that the family-Head Start interface is most appropriately viewed as a process of mutual adaptation that involves change on the part of both families and programs. Research, however, has neglected to document how Head Start program staff adapt to the characteristics, needs, and capabilities of the families they serve. What does it mean for a Head Start program to adapt to a family's cultural characteristics or self-determined goals for their children? When is adaptation inappropriate? More generally, what is the process by which Head Start programs evolve to accommodate emergent needs of the communities they serve?

Jean Layzer raised the following questions: What is family growth and how do we measure it? Are there models by which we can try to understand family change, particularly toward self-sufficiency and effective parenting? Only developmental models, she insisted, allow us to understand when and how a program might be having an effect on a family.

   • *Efforts to document the effects of Head Start need to incorporate parents' and other family members' perceptions of how the program has affected their behaviors, values, and opportunities.*

The roundtable members frequently noted that the family-level effects of Head Start are a relatively neglected story. One critical vantage point on this story is that of parents themselves. Using parents as informants may offer an initial step in a series of efforts to ascertain what works for whom in Head Start and in identifying aspects of family effects that the families themselves are concerned about. Oral histories from parents are an important addition to other efforts to document Head Start's efficacy: What aspects of Head Start do parents like, what would they like the program to offer them that it does not, and what do they believe their children are getting from Head Start? How has Head Start changed their relationships with their children—those in and those not in Head Start? How has Head Start enabled them to change the circumstances of their lives?

3

Recognizing the Diversity of Children and Families in Head Start

Head Start provides the first exposure to a school-like environment for children from a growing range of ethnic backgrounds, children for whom English is not the primary language, and migrant and immigrant children. Estimates suggest that 20 percent of the children enrolled in Head Start nationwide speak a language other than English (Kagan and Garcia, 1991). Preliminary findings from ACYF's Descriptive Study of Head Start Bilingual and Multicultural Program Services (see p. 21) reveal that: only about one-third of the programs had an enrollment characterized by a single, dominant language, the number of languages represented by the programs range from 1 to 32, and about 72 percent of the programs had enrollments of between 2 and 3 languages.

Immigration, mostly from non-European countries, is proceeding at such a rapid rate that half of the growth in the school-age population between 1990 and 2010 will be attributable to the children of immigrants (Board on Children, Youth, and Families, 1995). Head Start will see many of these children and their families before they enter kindergarten. Head Start also includes 24 programs for migrants that serve approximately 30,000 children, including infants and toddlers.

The implications of the changing ethnic and linguistic composition of the families and children that Head Start serves for the research community are profound. The population's diversity affects sampling strategies, alters views regarding the appropriateness of measures and assessments, and highlights the importance of connecting Head Start researchers with others in the field who are studying bilingualism and second language acquisition, for example.

This situation presents both an opportunity and a challenge to Head Start. On one hand, as a result of its long-standing efforts to serve a multicultural and linguistically diverse population, Head Start offers a natural laboratory for the study of these issues that lie at the intersection of ethnicity and development. As such, its program of research has the potential to be at the cutting edge of knowledge generation in this area. On the other hand, the empirical challenges involved in studying diverse populations are far from minor, and the political context in which this research occurs will place tremendous pressures on those engaged in this enterprise. With these tensions and possibilities in mind, the roundtable considered research on Head Start that is attuned to the diversity of the families it serves.

ISSUES FOR RESEARCH

The roundtable's discussion of research issues that are rooted in the ethnic and linguistic diversity of the Head Start population encompassed numerous topics, ranging from bilingual instruction to social development. Many of these topics are also discussed in a report of the Board on Children, Youth, and Families on cultural diversity and early education (Phillips and Crowell, 1994).

Instruction in Bilingual and Multilingual Classrooms

Questions regarding the language of instruction and interactions between language learning and content learning are understandably of great concern to Head Start staff. Staff members are increasingly confronted with the challenges of communicating with non-English-speaking children and their families; engaging in direct English language instruction; and encouraging the learning and social development of children whose language and culture they may not share. The English literacy of non-English-speaking Head Start parents, many of whom are experiencing growing pressures to enter the labor force, is also a matter of pressing concern to Head Start.

To increase the responsiveness of Head Start programs to the cultural and linguistic needs of the families they serve, in 1993 ACYF initiated a three-year Descriptive Study of Head Start Bilingual and Multicultural

Program Services. Its purpose is to identify the range of bilingual and multicultural services currently provided by all Head Start programs and to examine innovative service models. Phase I of the study involved a national survey of 2,006 Head Start programs to identify bilingual and multicultural services currently provided to children and families from bilingual and/or multicultural backgrounds. Phase II involved in-depth site visits to 30 Head Start programs that were identified as providing innovative bilingual/multicultural services. Preliminary results, suggesting that two-thirds of the programs serve children who are bilingual, point to the pressing need for further research in this area.

Although most of the literature on second language acquisition and bilingualism is focused on school-age children, there is a growing body of research on younger children. This emerging research has demonstrated, for example, that the acquisition of first and second languages is not a zero-sum process, as many parents appear to believe, but can be accomplished so that the development of both languages is supported.

In focusing on the diversity of some Head Start programs, Claude Goldenberg cautioned that we must not overlook the commonalities across diverse populations. There are common dreams that all families share for their children. Research could help to identify elements of this common ground that might provide a basis for bringing coherence and community to multicultural Head Start centers.

But many critical questions remain unanswered: When and how should English be introduced? Should native language instruction be phased out or retained as children learn English? What adjustments need to be made regarding instructional language for bilingual special education? What language characteristics and proficiencies of staff promote effective language and content instruction in multilingual classrooms?

Given the roundtable's focus on Head Start families, the tension between ensuring that young children retain their newly acquired competence in their native language and preparing them for what are typically English-only kindergartens was of great concern. For these children, the school transition process is very important, given that many Head Start children are likely to experience a shift from bilingual Head Start classrooms to unilingual kindergarten classrooms.

Members of the roundtable also stressed the importance of infusing questions about the quality and effectiveness of Head Start with the issue of culture: Which programs work best for whom and under what circumstances? The answers that emerge from research on monocultural Head Start programs may not hold true for multicultural programs.

Members of the roundtable also raised questions about the important competencies of support staff in Head Start who serve as mediators between children's home and school settings—a role that is made especially challenging when the language and culture of the home and the school are not similar. It is virtually impossible for any staff person to completely comprehend the language, cultural background, and family experiences of children from three or four widely divergent cultural backgrounds. What enables family support staff to be successful in bridging home and school environments? How are these staff best trained to accomplish this goal? How can parents and extended family members (e.g., grandparents) be involved in the program to make it more culturally diverse and relevant to their children's lives?

The Social Implications of Children's Language Environments

Beyond the core issues of language learning and instruction, the roundtable members examined the connection between language and social development. This issue is at the core of helping children to achieve social competence, an important goal of Head Start's comprehensive services (Stewart, 1994). Keeping this in mind, roundtable members explored questions such as: How does language affect social interactions in Head Start? Do children sort themselves by language? How does the language mix of the children in the program affect the development of social competencies? There is a dearth of research that addresses these issues in Head Start and in the fields of education and developmental psychology generally.

Available research suggests that, by fourth grade, social groupings and intergroup conflicts among children are strongly patterned around linguistic differences (Kagan, 1986). Although this situation is largely invisible in the preschool years, programmatic decisions about preschool teaching and activities should be developed with an eye to the child's future learning and social integration. There is a substantial need for longitudinal studies of the social experiences of children of different cultural and linguistic groups.

In considering the best pedagogical approaches for bilingual children, the interests and literacy views of parents are also very important (Goldenberg, Reese, and Gallimore, 1992). As part of the Descriptive Study of Head Start Bilingual and Multicultural Program Services, parents are interviewed about their language preferences. Preliminary results suggest that non-English-proficient parents tend to believe that young children can learn only one language well at a time and that they prefer English instruction because they equate it with school success.

Finally, the roundtable members considered the developmental dimensions of the 1994 amendment to the Head Start Act to create a new program of Head Start services for infants and toddlers. They raised issues regarding, for example, the impact that context has on early identity formation and the importance of linguistic continuity between home and Head Start for infants and toddlers who are just beginning to use language to communicate with adults.

The Significance of Parents' Background

Culture itself cannot be addressed as a simple variable. Studies of culture have to take into account the level of parents' schooling, families' economic status, and families' refugee or immigration status. The importance of parents' attained levels of formal education for their children's development has long been recognized. The roundtable's initial focus on family-level issues in Head Start, however, drew attention to several other, less well understood implications of parents' education levels. For example, the role of parents' own educational experiences in shaping their views of how children get ready for school, as well as the behaviors that derive from these views, are important to Head Start's efforts to integrate parents into its educational program.

Luis Laosa described how his efforts to discern interactions among culture and other variables have challenged the view that the important proxies for culture are race, ethnicity, and language. His recent work with Vietnamese, Cambodian, and Central American families in Head Start has identified the dominant influence of parental schooling and exposure to violence on these families and their children.

It also became evident to the roundtable members that the impact on children's and families' participation in Head Start programs of immigration and immigrant status is substantially less well understood than is the impact of parent education. Among the important issues identified are: How does immigrant status affect families' willingness to apply for Head Start? How does the immigration experience itself affect the needs of Head Start families? How do Head Start programs meet the needs of these families?

Migrant Families

Migrant families have unique characteristics and are not homogenous as a group. These families are highly dispersed and linguistically diverse; frequently, but temporarily, change family configurations; and gradually shift from migrant to "settled out" status. Their living conditions are not only unstable but also often pose serious safety and health hazards. Because of migrant families' special circumstances, their trajectory of involvement with Head Start is different from that of other families participating in Head Start programs. Providing services to these families is an exceedingly difficult task. Involving parents, for example, entails special provisions for transportation, extensive hours of program operation, and adaptation to unpredictable work schedules.

> *With regard to migrant centers—and indeed with regard to all Head Start programs—Carole Clarke highlighted two critical questions for research: What characteristics distinguish more and less effective support staff in the programs? What kinds of training will facilitate the staff's effectiveness in their work with a culturally diverse population?*

Many issues affecting migrant families warrant research attention. The issues are extremely complex, and the pragmatic demands of conducting research on migrant families with young children are daunting. A particularly salient issue concerns the programmatic implications of the climatic and economic unpredictability that characterizes the lives of migrant families.

ACYF will soon complete a descriptive study of Head Start migrant programs and the eligible migrant population. This study, A Descriptive

Study of the Characteristics of Families Served by Head Start Migrant Programs, will provide a profile of Head Start migrant families in the main migratory streams and generate information on unique issues related to serving migrant families through Head Start programs. The migrant study will document the availability and coordination of services for Head Start families during the migration process. It will also provide a national esti-mate of the number of children of migrant farmworkers who are eligible for Head Start services and of those children who are currently being served by Migrant Head Start programs. The findings from this study will effect policy decisions on Head Start migrant programs, as well as the new Early Head Start program for infants and toddlers; it is scheduled for completion in 1996.

A related set of issues concerns the developmental consequences of the constant disruptions in relations with caregivers that infants and tod-dlers experience as families migrate. For example, transferring medical records from one Head Start center to another as families migrate is logis-tically very difficult to coordinate given the uncertainty of the families' migratory pattern. Consequently, immunization records may be outdated, and this may have potential negative consequences for the child's health. Roundtable members questioned whether there are ways in which Head Start programs can offer greater continuity of care to these children.

Research on migrant families also needs to consider the highly disen-franchised status of these parents. What are the consequences when Head Start teaches decision-making skills to these families, offers them policy roles, and provides other experiences that enable them to assume legiti-mate authority roles? What are the ramifications of migrant families' sub-sequent involvement in the political process, or for their willingness and capacity to serve as advocates for their children as they become engaged in schools and other social institutions?

Gregg Powell pointed out that migrant children have so far been an invisible minority within the population of Head Start children. There is a dearth of research on what happens to migrant children in Head Start and as a result of Head Start.

NEXT STEPS FOR RESEARCH

The roundtable members identified five important directions for research in this area. They are grouped in terms of the three types of research agendas presented in Table 1.

Descriptive, Quality, and Outcome Agendas:

3-1. *To identify current instructional practices in mixed-language classrooms and to assess the effects of language mix within a group of children on their linguistic, cognitive, and social development,* conduct a descriptive study of classrooms in which two or three languages are represented among the children in varying configurations. For example, comparisons could be made between classrooms with approximately equal proportions of children per language and classrooms in which there is a dominant language and several other languages spoken by small numbers of children.

3-2. *To enhance understanding of how children's home and Head Start environments interact to affect their development and to assess the effects of language practices within Head Start on parents from diverse ethnic and linguistic groups,* supplement the descriptive study of classrooms and children with data on the children's home environments and parenting outcomes (e.g., the use of language at home, parents' beliefs about language acquisition and goals for language instruction in Head Start, parents' engagement with their children's schools and other community groups, and parents' aspirations for their children).

3-3. *To assess the extent to which language, migrant status, and immigrant status are barriers to participation in Head Start,* conduct a multisite community-based study of selection into Head Start that relies on a prospective design to determine which eligible families avail themselves of Head Start, why some do, and why others do not. Parents' knowledge of Head Start, perceptions of Head Start (including perceptions of eligibility), fit between parents' goals for children and their views of what Head Start offers, fears about possible ramifications of enrolling children in Head Start (e.g., deportation, loss of family control over children), and logistical and practical barriers are useful to consider.

Quality and Outcome Agendas:

3-4. *To ensure the most effective use of family support staff with linguistically and ethnically diverse families,* conduct an evaluation of current family support and home visit practices in a subsample of Head Start programs (migrant and nonmigrant) that serve large proportions of non-English-speaking and/or immigrant children. Such a study would benefit from documenting the characteristics and backgrounds (including training) of family support staff, observing what the staff do and how well they do it, and assessing family- and child-level effects. To extend the utility of this type of research, consideration might be given to a follow-up evaluation study in which highly effective family support staff are trained to serve as mentors for new staff.

Descriptive and Quality Agendas:

3-5. *To capture the processes by which Head Start programs adjust to the shifting demographics of families served and identify issues for future program intervention and research*, conduct a small, descriptive longitudinal study of several Head Start programs that are changing from serving a relatively homogeneous population of families to a relatively diverse population of families. By capturing a few such naturally occurring transitions and obtaining evidence about the issues involved in adapting to change from a range of vantage points (directors, teachers, support staff, parents, children), substantial insights can be gained into how programs adjust to change over time, including what works well, what doesn't, for whom, and under what conditions.

4

Examining Community–Head Start Collaborations

Head Start was conceptualized as a community action program, with a strong emphasis on local determination. It is unique as an intervention of national scope that, at the same time, is carefully tailored to the needs of each local community in which it exists. Head Start has brought tremendous resources and vitality to the communities it serves; its effectiveness, in turn, is partly dependent on the range of services and resources that surround it. Since Head Start is, by design, a program intended to facilitate coordination among other community services, there is a need to explore the strengths and weaknesses of the relationship between Head Start and other local programs (see Box 4).

It is commonly perceived that the array of community services and resources that surround Head Start today is more complex than was the case when the program was initiated. The United States is in the midst of significant reform efforts—in education, health care, and social services—that hold major, but unclear, implications for the community contexts of Head Start in the years ahead, as well as for the needs of Head Start families. It became evident to the roundtable members that Head Start faces a central challenge posed by its mandate to be a comprehensive, community-based program, on one hand, and by its need to make reasonable judgments about what it can be expected to accomplish in the context of contemporary poverty, on the other. This, in turn, raises questions about what it means to "involve" families in Head Start; the interdependence of Head

29

Box 4

To foster links with the community, the National Head Start Association has created four national partnerships with organizations that share the same mission and have similar infrastructures: the National PTA Association, the National Mental Health Association, the National Commission to Prevent Child Abuse, and Reading is Fundamental. In general, the goals of these partnerships are:

• to create a mechanism, at the national level, that provides programs with the technical assistance and concrete step-by-step guidance to create successful partnerships;

• to develop a substantive and long-term partnership;

• to establish the infrastructure needed to create partnerships that are long-term and self-generating; and

• to collect and disseminate data on promising practices.

Start and other community resources in efforts to achieve positive outcomes for children and families; and Head Start's role in relation to other organizations and resources in the community.

Because Head Start is reliant on community resources, it is profoundly affected by problems that have arisen in both urban and rural areas from the loss of community resources—notably economic resources—and the accompanying deterioration of the social fabric that holds communities together. The roundtable members focused their attention on the toll that community and family violence can take on Head Start programs and staff and on the families they serve, as well as on the mental health consequences for children and families of the combined impact of chronic poverty and violence. The prevailing notions of what a "good" Head Start program looks like and expectations of what such a program can accomplish may be increasingly inappropriate for many of the communities that Head Start now serves. Head Start's place in the configuration of community resources as it affects the program's capacity to meet families' needs, as well as the community-level effects of Head Start, has received minimal attention in recent research.

> Robin Jarret cautioned the roundtable about the difficulty of
> strengthening families in a social vacuum. Effective Head Start
> programs need to encourage parent coalitions, improve informal
> social controls and support systems, and help parents to establish
> a network of knowledge and resources. What are the
> contributions that Head Start's community action emphasis
> makes to these processes?

The questions regarding the effects of resource depletion and danger-
ous communities on Head Start are new and, as such, demand research
attention. For example, a 1994 General Accounting Office report on early
childhood programs reported that about one-fourth of Head Start programs, accounting for over 150,000 children, had difficulty getting help
from local health professionals in the community (U.S. General Accounting Office, 1994). These difficulties were due to: (1) the lack of available
resources in the community and (2) the reluctance of health professionals
to accept Medicaid reimbursements to treat Head Start children. It is
critical, then, to understand what Head Start faces in these communities,
to rethink notions of parent involvement and family support in this context, and to use this information to redefine the nature and scope of an
effective program in extremely deprived neighborhoods.

ISSUES FOR RESEARCH

Community Resources, Head Start Quality, and Community Impacts

The Advisory Committee on Head Start Quality and Expansion highlighted the importance of forging effective partnerships with key community institutions and programs as a critical component of creating a Head
Start for the 21st century (U.S. Department of Health and Human Services, 1993). It further noted that effective partnerships will require
changed roles at the federal, state, and local levels that must extend beyond Head Start to include a broad range of community institutions, from
child care services and schools—the focus of the Head Start Transition
Projects—to the private sector.

From the perspective of research, the roundtable members identified
three types of linkages that warrant examination: (1) Head Start families'

relations to other specialized services and community institutions that may either interfere with or contribute to Head Start's efforts to improve family well-being, (2) the nature and extent of Head Start's access to community resources that facilitate its capacity to offer families appropriate and high-quality services, and (3) the contribution of the presence of Head Start to the availability and quality of local resources and community institutions.

John Love cited the Free to Grow Project as an example of a partnership between community agencies and Head Start centers to promote substance abuse-free communities. The core of this effort is the attempt to strengthen the immediate environment of vulnerable children. This vulnerability, Love noted, is a function of a number of risk and protective factors identifiable in the child's environment.

Efforts to document the family-level effects of Head Start, as well as the ways in which families mediate the effects of Head Start on their children, rarely consider the influence of Head Start in the context of other resources and services in the community that are often available to its families. Estimates of the effects of Head Start need to consider the constellation of other community-level influences—positive and negative—on the families it serves. The issue is not one of estimating Head Start's effects *net* of other services, but of examining variation in Head Start's effects as a function of the context of the community resources in which it operates. When do surrounding resources undermine, or encourage, the capacity of Head Start to produce beneficial outcomes in its children and families?

The quality of services that Head Start provides to its families depends increasingly on its fit with other institutions—formal and informal—in the network of resources that serve the same families. Today, it is increasingly difficult to meet all of the needs of impoverished families in the context of full-time employment by low-income mothers, growing needs for mental health services, calls to improve family literacy, and rising community violence, to name a few contemporary pressures on Head Start. Indeed, the roundtable members discussed the possibility of stretching basic conceptions of high-quality Head Start programs to encompass aspects of collaboration with other community institutions and to assume greater responsibility for ensuring that the needs of the families it serves are not only identified, but also addressed. Among the questions raised: What features of Head Start enable it to forge productive linkages with other community resources? What opportunities exist for collaborative needs assessments and staff training? How can the lessons that Head Start has already learned about providing comprehensive services be shared with a broader array of community institutions?

Sara Rosenbaum discussed the need to find ways to connect Head Start centers with new ventures in managed health care. She stressed the need to study the relationship between Head Start centers and local health management organizations, and to develop models and precedents for collaboration between Head Start and health management organizations.

A respected effort aimed at documenting the effects of Head Start on the community was conducted 25 years ago (Kirschner Associates Inc., 1970). Field research was conducted in a national sample of 58 communities with full-year Head Start programs and 7 communities with little exposure to Head Start. The most promising conclusion of the report was that Head Start had been instrumental in fostering some fundamental changes in communities. The reported changes included increased involvement of the poor in decision-making capacities with local institutions, increased employment among the indigenous population as paraprofessionals, greater responsiveness of schools to the comprehensive needs of the children in their communities, and modification of health services and practices to serve the poor more effectively (see Box 5).

Today, the socioeconomic environment of impoverished families is in tremendous flux. As a result, community changes such as those found in the Kirschner study may be difficult to replicate. Furthermore, in the context of serious fiscal constraints in many communities, these types of changes may prove more difficult to accomplish than in the late 1960s when resources were more plentiful and the nation rallied behind the War on Poverty. At a minimum, any effort to identify community-level effects of Head Start would need to reconsider the outcomes that are both important to assess and amenable to measurement.

Box 5

The Kirschner report documented the following community-level effects of Head Start:

- In one southern community, the public health institution desegregated its waiting room and opened the facilities one evening a week; families in poverty increased their use of this health care resource.

- A midwestern school system employed indigenous teacher aides in poor neighborhoods to tutor children after school.

- In Appalachia, a visiting nurse program was established to provide routine nursing care to the sick.

- A school system in a northern industrial city developed an after-school recreational activity program in its lowest-income neighborhoods.

- A group of Head Start parents formed a consumer cooperative that purchased fresh fruits and vegetables in bulk and distributed them to families in inner-city neighborhoods.

Families in Violent Homes and Communities

Despite growing evidence of children's extensive exposure to violence in the community and in the home, research on this issue is in its infancy. This area of research was recently the topic of a major National Research Council report, *Understanding Child Abuse and Neglect* (National Research Council, 1993). It is also the subject of a major study, conducted under the auspices of the Board on Children, Youth, and Families, on assessing family violence interventions that is scheduled for completion in 1996.

We lack basic statistics on the prevalence with which preschool-age children in this country witness violence, are threatened, or are the direct victims of violence. Similarly, representative data on the frequency or chronicity of young children's exposure to violence are unavailable. This is due in part to the absence of reliable methods for measuring exposure to violence in young children, particularly exposure that stops short of direct physical harm to the child (e.g., Taylor, Zuckerman, Harik, and McAlister Groves, 1994). Efforts to understand the consequences of exposure to chronic community and family violence are necessarily limited by the reality that efforts to define and document the phenomenon are in their early stages (Osofsky, 1995). In the absence of a taxonomy of *kinds* of violence, however, and a more detailed understanding of its epidemiology, it is exceedingly difficult to estimate the magnitude of the problem and to consider ways in which Head Start centers can move to confront it.

Head Start nevertheless serves a growing population of children who are exposed to violence, sometimes frequently and chronically, and for whom the consequences are abundantly evident. The roundtable members focused on issues that enlist Head Start in efforts to identify promising approaches for helping children and their families cope with exposure to violence. If Head Start becomes part of an effort to develop effective prevention programs for young children exposed to violence, then it will also have the opportunity to contribute to the development of appropriate outcomes for tracking the progress of these children. Also, the roundtable discussed the important effect that violence may have on selection into Head Start and the dearth of research on the effects of exposure to violence on parenting and caregiving—a target for both intervention and adaptation of traditional approaches to parent involvement in Head Start.

> Barry Zuckerman identified two areas that merit research attention: measures of exposure to violence and intervention programs in Head Start. As researchers begin to unravel the developmental consequences of children's exposure to violence, there is an urgent need to develop markers of exposure that can be used by the range of adults, including Head Start teachers, who work with young children.

The provision of services in the context of violent communities is a topic with immense practical significance and about which little is known. Among the questions raised: How does the presence of violence in the community change Head Start programs? How do programs cope with violence and what supports do they need? What, for example, are the implications of violence for carrying out home visit requirements? What is the impact of violence on parents and their capacity to parent? What adaptations in strategies for involving parents, such as using workshops on *safety* rather than on *parenting* to draw parents into Head Start, suggest themselves in this context? It was noted that some Head Start programs in some communities cannot recruit teachers because of the attendant dangers of working in the neighborhoods in which the programs are located.

Joy Osofsky noted that young children exposed to violence tend to behave like adults who have experienced post-traumatic stress syndrome: they are unable to concentrate, experience anxiety and phobias, reexperience the event in their play, show blunt affect, and exhibit social withdrawal or increased aggression. These children also experience language delay, developmental regression, and have changed perceptions of the future.

Given the immense demands that these circumstances place on Head Start, some roundtable members pointed out that the issue of violence offers a very significant context within which to examine productive linkages between Head Start and other community resources. One roundtable member noted, for example, that 46 percent of Head Start programs have access to mental health professionals "on call" only; most lack crisis teams and intervention plans for dealing with children who have been exposed to violence. In the workshops, the roundtable members learned about collaborations with police departments that appear to hold promise for bolstering the resources that are typically available to Head Start programs.

Because Head Start draws its staff from the communities that it serves, a central issue discussed concerns the large number of Head Start staff members who themselves witness violence and are the victims of violence. These staff are not only caring for children who have been exposed to violence, but are also struggling with the same issues in their own lives. Models of staff training tailored to issues of violence and its mental health ramifications are greatly needed.

Jane Knitzer urged researchers to examine the ways in which Head Start centers deal with mental health issues. How do they link with other community professionals and programs? Can we identify some promising programmatic strategies (e.g., preschool mental health teams)?

NEXT STEPS FOR RESEARCH

Community Resources and Effects

The roundtable members identified three important directions for research in this area, grouped in terms of the three types of research agendas presented in Table 1.

Descriptive, Quality, and Outcome Agendas:

4-1. *To document critical family-level effects of Head Start that bear on parents' capacity to mobilize community resources for their children,* initiate a measurement development effort focused on this dimension of parent functioning. Important components of this parental role include: parental awareness of community resources, knowledge about how to access these resources, and the actual use of this knowledge on behalf of their children.

4-2. *To assess the impact of differing constellations of community resources on what Head Start is able to offer families, how well it provides these services, and with what effects on families and children,* several strategies could be employed. These strategies would lay the stage for a more extensive study focused on how communities affect Head Start.

First, a pilot study of several Head Start communities, deliberately selected to represent some that are relatively resource- rich and some that are relatively resource poor, could contribute to developing and refining a methodology for categorizing communities in ways that are meaningful for Head Start (e.g., institutional resources, specialized services, training resources, availability of specialists who can volunteer time to Head Start, private-sector resources). Such a study could also begin to assess how and why Head Start utilizes or fails to utilize these resources.

Second, a small sample of Head Start centers selected to represent high- and low-quality programs serving similar populations could be compared to obtain preliminary data on their differing access to and strategies for availing themselves of community resources. A pilot study of this nature could begin to identify the community conditions under which Head Start is able to provide high-quality care.

Third, in light of ongoing extensive state- and local-level experimentation with welfare reform, health care reform, and early education, it may be possible to take advantage of natural experiments at a small number of Head Start sites that are undergoing appreciable shifts in available resources or major reconfigurations of available resources. A longitudinal design would be essential for such a study, as would extensive reliance on ethnographic methodologies aimed at capturing shifting community resources and their effects on Head Start.

Descriptive and Outcome Agendas:

4-3. *To update prior findings regarding the community-level effects of Head Start,* conduct a replication and extension of the Kirschner Associates study of community impacts of Head Start. As part of this type of initiative, it would be important to reconsider the outcomes that are important to assess in today's community contexts. Examples of community-level factors to capture are community resources, community cohesiveness, opportunities for citizen decision-making, and institutional responsiveness to the needs of poor families.

Violence

The roundtable members identified three important directions for research in this area:

Descriptive Agenda:

4-4. *To obtain a current profile of the prevalence and chronicity with which children and staff in Head Start are exposed to community and domestic violence and to increase public awareness of the contemporary conditions under which Head Start must operate,* consider opportunities for appending a supplemental interview focused on these issues to staff and family surveys that are in the field or being contemplated. Staff, for example, could be asked to identify the extent and degree to which children in their care exhibit behaviors that have been linked to post-traumatic stress disorders in children (e.g., reenacting violent events, social withdrawal, diminished range of affect, startle responses, and hypervigilance).

4-5. *To begin to ascertain the effects of exposure to violence on Head Start families and staff, to gain an understanding of how staff and parents view Head Start's role in this context, and to identify appropriate targets for intervention,* conduct a qualitative, interview-based study of staff, teachers, and parents focused on these issues, perhaps linked with the proposed interview on prevalence of exposure. In addition, teachers could provide valuable insights into how children exposed to violence behave, learn, and get along with peers and staff in classrooms. How are Head Start programs, staff, and families currently coping with exposure to violence? What are the programmatic effects, emotional effects, effects on family and staff recruitment, and effects on how programs interact with parents and on parent involvement and home visits? Who appears to be coping well and why? What are some strategies that staff have developed to cope with children who have been exposed to violence? What types of training and support would staff and parents like to receive? If assessed over time, answers to these questions could begin to provide insights into the evolving process of coping with violence.

Descriptive and Outcome Agendas:

4-6. *To highlight the potential role of Head Start as a locus for violence prevention efforts and to develop program models in this area that are tailored to the Head Start population (staff and families),* conduct a demonstration project at Head Start sites that are affected by moderate and high rates of community violence. Among the innovative efforts that could be examined are staff training strategies, ties to local police departments, therapeutic models, development of crisis teams, and various combinations of approaches (e.g., joint training for Head Start staff and local police in which expertise is exchanged). A critical element of such a project would be the development of evaluation criteria and measures aimed at identifying effective preventive intervention programs that are amenable to implementation within or in collaboration with Head Start.

5

Head Start Families in a Changing Economic Landscape

Head Start was launched during an era when maternal employment, even among the poor, was far less prevalent than it is today. Evidence regarding long-term welfare dependence had not yet become an issue, and there was greater public tolerance for nonemployment among mothers with young children eligible for Aid to Families with Dependent Children (AFDC). Contemporary rates of employment and pressures toward labor force participation for low-income mothers, including those with very young children, contrast sharply with this earlier portrait. Among children under age 5 in families with household incomes below $15,000, 29 percent are being raised by two employed parents or by a working single parent, typically the mother (Brayfield et al., 1993).

A large share of parents in Head Start families are also employed. More than one-third of Head Start children have at least one parent who works full time; another 15 percent have parents who work part time or seasonally, and 5 percent of children have parents who are in school or training (U.S. Department of Health and Human Services, 1993). In contrast, employed single-parent families are underrepresented in Head Start (Hofferth, 1994). Although Head Start programs currently have legislative authority to use funds for full-day services, administrative policies over the past several years have discouraged such practices (U.S. Department of Health and Human Services, 1993). Only 6.5 percent of Head Start children were served for 8 hours a day in 1991-1992. However, in the context of welfare-to-work initiatives, the recently amended Head Start Act (1994) contains a provision that requires the Department of Health and Human Services to conduct a study of the extent to which Head Start programs are addressing the need for services during a full working day or full calendar year among eligible low-income families with preschool children.

A hallmark of Head Start has been its focus on addressing the developmental needs of young children and involving parents as partners in this process. Today, as the needs of parents increasingly involve full-time work and as mothers in poverty are mandated to work, meeting parents' needs takes on new meaning. Not surprisingly, in a 1990 survey conducted by the National Head Start Association, parents most often listed the need for extended hours and days of operation of Head Start centers as an area that needed improvement.

> *Janet Swartz informed the roundtable that more than 90 percent of the caseworkers in her research program mentioned employment when asked to identify the greatest needs of the families with whom they work and highlighted the importance of understanding the role of case management within Head Start.*

Head Start also plays a significant role as a employer of Head Start parents. One-third of Head Start employees are former Head Start parents. And several Head Start programs are involved in extensive parent literacy and job training initiatives. These sets of issues surrounding Head Start's role in the economic dimension of poor families' lives—as employer, a site for job training, and a source of care for the children of working parents—surfaced repeatedly in the presentations and discussions among the roundtable members.

As welfare reform at the state level affects a growing share of Head Start-eligible families, pressures on the program to articulate its relation not only to parents' childrearing responsibilities, but also to their responsibilities (and requirements) to prepare for and sustain paid employment, will mount.

*Randale Valenti noted that, since welfare reform is unmistakably
on the table politically, the pressing question is: What are the
challenges associated with integrating Head Start with various
parents' employment scenarios?*

ISSUES FOR RESEARCH

The vision of Head Start is to launch children on a trajectory of school success and social competence that will, among other goals, reduce welfare dependence in the next generation. Today, however, parents living in poverty have also become the focus of developmental programs aimed at redirecting the trajectories of their lives away from dependence and toward economic self-sufficiency. The lives of Head Start children, as a result, are set in motion along two paths simultaneously—their own developmental path and that of their parents—both of which are being heavily orchestrated by public policies. As a pivotal institution in these families' lives, what possibilities are available to Head Start to redefine what it means to be a two-generational program in this new policy context? How can research help to identify these possibilities?

In addressing these questions, members of the roundtable first acknowledged that research that focuses on the changing economic landscape of Head Start-eligible families will confront a central tension concerning the program's fundamental goals. Head Start was *not* designed primarily to meet the child care needs of full-time, full-year employed parents. The relatively high quality of Head Start programs, compared with full-day community-based child care centers (see Layzer et al., 1993), may actually depend on their circumscribed hours of operation and clear focus on the developmental needs of children (as distinct from the employment-related needs of their parents). Yet even the Advisory Committee on Head Start Quality and Expansion noted that "Head Start can no longer continue to be a half-day program for children in those families that need full-day, full-year services" (U.S. Department of Health and Human Services, 1993: 47).

In light of the tensions that surround this topic and recent examinations of pertinent policies by the Board on Children, Youth, and Families (see its two 1995 reports, *New Findings on Children, Families, and Economic Self-Sufficiency* and *Child Care for Low-Income Families*), the roundtable members identified three issues that warrant the immediate scrutiny of research: (1) Head Start's role as a training ground and job site for the parents of enrolled children; (2) the implications of the new economic pressures on Head Start families for parent involvement strategies; and (3) effective approaches to providing high-quality, cost-effective, full-day services for the Head Start population. This last effort is an important step toward complying with the 1994 Head Start Act's provision of studying the full-day need for Head Start services. Hence, the exploration of new program options, which offer the opportunity to bridge the gap that still separates the child care and Head Start traditions in this country, was an overriding theme of the roundtable's discussions.

Head Start as a Catalyst for Employment

Few dispute that provisions to support the care of young children while their parents prepare for employment must be a central component of any welfare-to-work initiative. Although the benefits that may be provided are often meager and short term—a far cry from the vision of Head Start— those who craft job training and employment policies for families in poverty know that connections must be made to child care policy. Ironically, those who create policies for the early care and education of children in poverty are only now beginning to recognize the value of making connections to training and employment policy.

The roundtable heard from several pioneers in this area, including those who are involved with Head Start's family service centers,[1] the founders of Project Match (see Box 3), and researchers involved in the evaluation of the Comprehensive Child Development Centers.[2] In addition, the roundtable had the benefit of the work of the Advisory Committee on Head Start Quality and Expansion, which gave special focus to parent literacy training in the context of Head Start. Based on this input, several issues that could benefit from new research were identified.

The first concerns the intersection between welfare policy and Head

---

[1] The goal of the Head Start Family Service Center Demonstration Projects is to ameliorate the interrelated problems of illiteracy, substance abuse, and unemployment, which limit the capacity of many Head Start families to achieve self-sufficiency. This project is conducted in collaboration with local community programs.

[2] The Comprehensive Child Development Program (CCDP) is a demonstration program funded by ACYF in 1989 to provide comprehensive care to low-income families at 24 sites throughout the country. The program aims to improve the cognitive, socioemotional, and physical development of low-income children.

Start policy. As a starting point, it would be beneficial to obtain basic information on the number and characteristics of Head Start families who also receive income support from the Aid to Families with Dependent Children program. More generally, it would be useful to gain a better understanding of the sources of income (e.g., earned, AFDC, child support, Medicaid, and other contributions) that constitute the economic resources of Head Start families. Because the greatest pressures toward labor force participation (and extensive participation) are likely to fall on the AFDC population, Head Start programs that serve large numbers of these families will be among the first child-focused programs to feel the impact of state and federal welfare reform experiments.

Second, efforts within Head Start to stretch parent involvement to embrace literacy and job training initiatives have generated important new insights into what it takes to successfully promote economic self-sufficiency. For example, progress, like development in general, is seldom linear or entirely predictable. These families and those who work with them experience alternating periods of progress and setbacks. As a result, flexibility around the sequencing and timing of activities (e.g., work first, then school), in the context of clear expectations and rewards for moving along a clear sequence of steps (e.g., register for a Graduate Equivalency Degree program, show up on time for the classes, take the exam), appears to be key to helping families with young children make the transition to employment. Another insight concerned the fact that these families do not have networks into the job market; not only do they need preparation for jobs, but also specific assistance finding jobs. Even more important, but challenging, is the task of helping these families *keep* jobs. Finally, the parenting role appears to be a powerful incentive that drives work effort. Programs that build on this, for example, by rewarding being on time with the child's drop-off at Head Start and then shifting to rewards for work-related timeliness, or developing work skills by training a parent to be the newsletter editor for their Head Start center, appear to have greater odds of success.

Third, not only is Head Start a locus for job preparation, but it also has historically served as a source of employment for low-income parents. In this context, the roundtable members raised several questions for research: What are the career trajectories of the parents who are employed by Head Start both prior to and after working in the program? What are their earnings trajectories? What barriers presently militate against the successful translation of employment in Head Start to potentially more lucrative employment in other settings? How does parent employment in Head Start affect their children's (those in and not in Head Start) motivation in school and aspirations for the future? Research that approaches these parents as workers and as models of employment for their children should be viewed as integral to the goals of Head Start.

Parent Involvement in the New Economic Context

Schooling, job training, and employment inevitably restrict the options for parent involvement that are realistically available to Head Start families. For all parents, the demands of the workplace are increasingly impinging on the time and energy that they can make available for their children. Parents who are raising children in the context of poverty are not immune from these pressures. Indeed, given the nonstandard work schedules and inflexibility that tend to characterize low-wage work (see Hofferth, 1994), they may feel these pressures even more acutely than other families. Models of parent involvement that were developed in an era when the majority of low-income mothers did not work require reexamination in this era when economic viability entails substantial work effort and expectations about poor families entail job preparation and employment regardless of the number and ages of children at home.

The roundtable members heard evidence gathered from interviews with Head Start families about their experiences, which highlighted the numerous barriers to parent involvement that currently exist. A prominent issue is the lack of adequate child care for the siblings of Head Start children and during non-Head Start hours, which is when parent meetings often occur. Mental health problems such as depression, health problems and disabilities, and work and school schedules were also frequently cited as barriers to parent involvement.

Susan Young suggested doing case studies of parents and their initial encounters with Head Start for the purpose of identifying life circumstances that support or discourage parent involvement.

In this context, the design and deployment of effective parent involvement strategies warrant careful examination. One set of issues pertains to the strategies that are available to staff for involving parents. These stragegies presently encompass a range of rather different activities:

1. Participation, mainly of parents, in the governance of the Head Start center in which their children are (or have been) involved;

2. Participation of family members on a voluntary or paid basis as assistants or teachers working with children at Head Start centers;

3. Participation of family members in community actions designed to improve conditions of life for poor families with young children;

4. Creation of mutual support groups among Head Start families who can call upon assistance from each other as the need arises; and

5. Provision to Head Start parents (and other adult family members) of information and training that can enable them to be more effective in caring for and interacting with their children.

Research is needed, nevertheless, to distinguish forms of parent involvement that are now *most* likely to enhance the development of young children growing up in poor families—increasingly with employed parents—and to identify a broader range of ways to involve parents, including those focused on literacy and job skills, than is currently the norm within Head Start. A central challenge involves identifying strategies that can be tailored, first, to the other demands that characterize parents' lives and, second, to their motivation and capacity to get involved. The importance of examining strategies that take into consideration the ways in which family members other than mothers (e.g., fathers, grandparents) participate in the lives of their children was of special interest to the roundtable members. For example, the roundtable members highlighted the importance of the role that grandparents and community elders play in childrearing, especially in multigenerational families. Grandparents are particularly important as primary caregivers with teenage parents. Research is needed to identify promising avenues for involving these individuals in Head Start.

James Levine argued that programs again and again have demonstrated that fathers can be involved in Head Start programs and that, when they are, there are benefits to the child and to the family. He urged the roundtable to rethink the problem of establishing parent involvement, to bring in the whole family.

Because new strategies will be only as effective as the staff who implement them, there is a critical need to reorient staff development and training to highlight strategies for working with irregularly involved parents, including exploration of the staffs' feelings about the parents they are trying to engage. Approaches that (1) encourage first steps, (2) offer meaningful forms of participation to parents with different capabilities and different circumstances, and (3) establish relationships of mutual respect with parents and staff warrant careful documentation and study.

Finally, and especially prominent in the roundtable's discussions about new strategies for parent involvement, were concerns about the social realities that even the most creative approaches to parent involvement now confront. What else is needed in order to ensure effective parent involvement? Child care is a clear and relatively straightforward need. Mental health and substance abuse services may be another element of effective parent involvement strategies at some, if not many, Head Start sites. Migrant Head Start programs have faced daunting challenges in offering opportunities for parent involvement and might be an especially useful source of ideas for overcoming some of the community- and family-based conditions that militate against effective, sustained parent involvement.

Full-Time Needs and Part-Day Programs

It is becoming increasingly evident that many Head Start programs are inaccessible to single employed parents who are nevertheless eligible to enroll their children. Head Start predominantly serves eligible children of nonworking parents and those who are in education and training programs prior to employment (Brayfield et al., 1993; Hofferth, 1994). This suggests that Head Start runs the risk of being beyond the reach of precisely those families in poverty who are struggling to do everything right as now defined by prevailing attitudes about dependence and work. Furthermore, the Head Start and child care communities have joined to share resources and construct effective bridges across their respective services in only a handful of exemplary sites. Keenly aware of these circumstances, the Advisory Committee on Head Start Quality and Expansion called on researchers to study efforts aimed at improving coordination and collaboration across Head Start and other early childhood programs in local communities.

To learn more about effective means of providing for child care that meets comparable quality standards as Head Start programs and provides employment opportunities for family members, ACYF is conducting an evaluation of the Head Start-Family Child Care Demonstration project. The goal of this project is to provide Head Start services through family child care homes. Preliminary findings suggest that Head Start services equivalent to those of center-based programs can be provided in a family child care home.

Again, the roundtable members identified a cluster of research issues that bear on the challenges arising from pressures for extensive labor force participation by poor parents. How individual children are distributed across the various prekindergarten and child care programs that now exist in most localities remains largely a mystery. Given an illogical system, a significant policy issue exists regarding the equity with which comparably poor children have access to and receive care that meets the high standards of Head Start and that provides a comparable range of services. The factors that impinge on children's selection into Head Start, the number and characteristics of children who do not enter Head Start and the quality of care they receive in the absence of Head Start, represent epidemiological and descriptive data needs that the roundtable members viewed as crucial to fulfilling many of Head Start's current goals.

To the extent that Head Start is being encouraged to consider collaborative models, its accompanying research enterprise must also be collaborative. One somewhat obvious manifestation of a more collaborative research agenda would be the inclusion, where appropriate, of non-Head Start programs in samples for Head Start research initiatives. The roundtable members were highly cognizant of the great divide that now characterizes the research literatures on child care, education, mental health, pediatrics, Head Start, and other related disciplines and was supportive of efforts aimed at bridging the disciplinary divides.

Perhaps the most useful target for research aimed at promoting continuity of care for Head Start children as their parents move into full-time jobs is the identification of feasible and cost-effective strategies for providing high-quality, full-day, full-year early childhood services. Because many of the factors that have deterred this goal have been financial and logistical in nature, effective research in this area will necessarily involve a number of technical and economic considerations. What approaches to linking funding mechanisms across various subsidy programs have served to protect families from arbitrary discontinuities in care? What regulatory and other top-down policy constraints need to be overcome to enable existing programs to establish effective linkages? What costs and benefits are associated with differing approaches to covering the full hours of parental employment, including those that derive from within Head Start and those that are based elsewhere? What have we learned from the growing share of Head Start programs that have used various strategies to provide full-day services? What have we learned from existing efforts to extend Head Start-type services to other child care programs in local communities? What other out-of-home settings have 4-year-olds enrolled in Head Start attended prior to Head Start? While children are in Head Start, are they also attending other forms of child care? How do the practices and quality of these other settings compare to the environment of Head Start classrooms? What are their differential effects on child development?

NEXT STEPS FOR RESEARCH

The roundtable members identified five important directions for research in this area; grouped in terms of the three types of research agendas presented in Table 1.

Descriptive Agenda:

5-1. *To obtain an accurate portrait of reliance on public assistance and of the income sources that are available to children in Head Start families* (including those provided by noncustodial fathers and other family members), consider appending a supplemental interview focused on these issues to family surveys that are in the field or being planned. Ideally, these questions could be asked repeatedly (every 6 months) during a family's involvement with Head Start to capture the dynamics of family income and employment in this population. Consideration could also be given to obtaining comparable data on a sample of Head Start-eligible but nonenrolled families to determine whether there are systematic differences between the income sources of enrolled and nonenrolled families living in poverty.

5-2. *To document the effects of Head Start on parents' employment opportunities and career and earnings trajectories*, conduct a prospective, longitudinal study of parents in a random sample of Head Start centers—some of whom obtain jobs within Head Start and some of whom obtain work elsewhere or do not obtain employment—and follow them through their early career moves. With careful documentation of selection effects, such a study could document Head Start's long-standing role as a "leg up" for many low-income parents into the labor force. In addition to documenting the work and earnings pathways of families in poverty, it would be beneficial to assess effects on family resources, family stability, child care arrangements, and child outcomes.

Descriptive, Quality, and Outcome Agendas:

5-3. *To continue to advance Head Start's efforts to provide high-quality, effective literacy and job training to its participating families*, develop a systematic program of demonstration and evaluation research on different approaches to this type of two-generation program. What are the most critical ingredients of successful programs, defined in terms of outcomes for parents and children? Do these critical elements differ based on the characteristics of the families being served? Are the elements that promote the successful completion of training programs the same as those that enable parents to sustain employment?

5-4. *To obtain a current profile of the range and intensity of parent involvement strategies currently being used in Head Start, and to provide a base for subsequent research on the effectiveness of different approaches with various families*, support a descriptive study of current parent involvement practices in Head Start that relies on multiple informants and multiple methods of data collection (surveys, interviews, participant observations). Ideally, such a study would be designed to capture a "year in the life of" the family-Head Start interface, starting with recruitment and enrollment and continuing through several months after graduation from Head Start. Including programs that have experience with involving fathers, grandparents, and foster parents would be extremely worthwhile given the changing family demographics of Head Start children and the critical need to reassess current assumptions about *whom* to involve in Head Start.

5-5. *To identify cost-effective approaches to providing for the full-time, full-year care needs of a growing share of Head Start families*, conduct an economic analysis of differing strategies for providing full-day, full-year services. Among the models that are most pertinent to Head Start are those that compare the costs of differing approaches to full-day Head Start, such as wraparound programs, to the costs of supplementing the quality and comprehensiveness of existing, community-based child care programs—both family-based and center-based. To provide the most useful data regarding the comparative pros and cons of differing approaches, such a study would need to document both costs and benefits, including those that accrue over time (e.g., identification of health and developmental delays that can compromise early school achievement, parents' successful transition from welfare to employment, reduced behavioral problems in school).

6

Extending the Benefits of
Local Innovation

Throughout the presentations and discussions of family-level research on Head Start, the roundtable members were impressed by the high level of local innovation. They learned about creative strategies for involving all parents, encouraging the participation of fathers, addressing community violence, providing family literacy and self-sufficiency programs, teaching in the context of multilingual classrooms, and linking Head Start with other community services. They were also concerned, however, about the dearth of opportunities for sharing the insights gained from innovative practices across Head Start programs and among the many participants in the early childhood service sector. These two contradictory impressions led the roundtable members to give careful thought to how the research community might assist with understanding the process of local innovation within Head Start and then extending this experience to other programs.

The report of the Advisory Panel for the Head Start Evaluation Design Project (U.S. Department of Health and Human Services, 1990) reflected similar interest in ensuring that research captures not only mainstream practices in Head Start, but also the innovative program strategies that are emerging, often in the context of small-scale demonstration projects. Similarly, the Advisory Committee on Head Start Quality and Expansion (U.S. Department of Health and Human Services, 1993) refers frequently to promising innovations and strategies that are proliferating among individual Head Start programs, yet are not shared with others.

The roundtable members concurred that efforts to transfer the insights gained from local innovations need to be an integral aspect of any future research agenda on Head Start. The ingredients that enable programs to be innovative, local uses of research to facilitate innovation, and the process of extending effective strategies to a wider network of Head Start programs all require careful documentation. To promote such innovative activities, the roundtable members identified a set of questions—all amenable to exploration by research—that need to be understood if the benefits of local innovation are to be exported to a broader network of Head Start programs:

- Why has the transfer of local innovation not occurred? What are the current obstacles to its taking place?
- How and to what extent do Head Start programs currently acquire knowledge about effective practices?
- How do they adapt such knowledge to their local needs and conditions?
- How and to what extent do they use research, including self-evaluations and local needs assessments, to inform the change processes entailed by innovation?
- How do programs institutionalize effective innovations so that the changes remain in place when specific projects (and funding) end?
- What enables programs to be innovative and entrepreneurial? What resources do these programs have access to? What skills and orientations appear to be essential?
- Can the skills essential for importing and implementing innovative ideas be taught? Can essential resources be replicated?
- What would enable innovative programs to share the effective and ineffective strategies they have tried and the lessons they have learned with other sites?
- What conditions enable Head Start programs to learn from the innovations of other programs? What is the best mode of communication across sites with respect to strategies?

If these issues could be addressed effectively within Head Start, a challenging but very promising next step would involve combining successful, innovative practices from child care, school-based, special education, family support, and other forms of early childhood and family-focused interventions. This challenge calls for research that would facilitate the identification and dissemination of innovations not only for Head Start, but also for other areas of early childhood service delivery.

Unlike the previous chapters of this report that offer specific examples of the types of research issues that would be profitable for Head Start to pursue, the discussions of knowledge exchange regarding innovative practices cut across each of the substantive topics for which specific research ideas were generated. For example, innovative practices in any of a number of areas could provide the focus for a companion program of research focused specifically on the questions outlined above: (1) creative responses to the infusion of cultural and linguistic diversity that Head Start programs are experiencing, (2) ways of coping with being situated in violent neighborhoods and with the behavioral and mental health problems that these neighborhoods can generate, and (3) innovative approaches to assisting Head Start families who are striving to increase their work effort.

In effect, the roundtable's discussions of program innovation addressed the central role of research within Head Start. Although one critical mission of Head Start research is to document the effects of the program—the public accountability role—the roundtable members were also keenly interested in the role of research as a tool that directors and other program staff can use to understand and modify their own practices. Research, in this instance, holds the promise of becoming a partner in staffs' efforts to make their programs more responsive to the changing needs of the families they serve.

Keenly aware of the important role that the synergy between researchers and program directors plays in conducting research, ACYF recently funded four university-based Head Start Quality Research Centers that will undertake, in partnership with Head Start grantees and ACYF, site-specific and cross-cutting research projects on Head Start quality program practices. These projects will include longitudinal studies of Head Start children and their families to examine how factors related to the quality of Head Start program practices affect the developmental progress of children and overall family functioning.

While hopeful about utilizing research for self-improvement within the Head Start community, the roundtable members were neither sanguine nor naive about the many pressures that militate against this. Notable are a shortage of local capacity to collect and use data at the local program level, prevailing suspicions about whether research *can* be a useful tool in program design and innovation, and time and resource constraints on all programs.

Nevertheless it is fitting, precisely because of these many barriers, to conclude this report with a discussion of the role of research in highlighting and extending the benefits of local innovation. Without attention to how Head Start's research agenda can incorporate the study and extension of local innovation, the insights gained from the myriad research issues identified in these pages will have only a modest chance of affecting the quality of services that families receive when they become part of the Head Start community.

References

Board on Children and Families (now Board on Children, Youth, and Families)
  1995   Immigrant children and their families: Issues for research and policy. *The Future of Children* 5(2):72-89.
Brayfield, A., S.G. Deich, and S. Hofferth
  1993   *Caring for Children in Low-Income Families: A Substudy of the National Child Care Survey, 1990.* A National Association for the Education of Young Children Study conducted by the Urban Institute. Washington, D.C.: Urban Institute Press.
Goldenberg, C., L. Reese, and R. Gallimore
  1992   Effects of literacy materials from school on Latino children's home experiences and early reading achievement. *American Journal of Education* 100(4):497-536.
Hofferth, S.
  1994   Who enrolls in Head Start? A demographic analysis of Head Start-eligible children. *Early Childhood Research Quarterly* 9:243-268.
Huston, A.C., V.C. McLoyd, and C. Garcia Coll
  1994   Children and poverty: Issues in contemporary research. *Child Development* 65:275-282.
Kagan, S.
  1986   Cooperative learning and sociocultural factors in schooling. In Bilingual Education Office, California State Department of Education, *Beyond Language: Social and Cultural Factors in Schooling Language Minority Students.* California State University, Los Angeles.
Kagan, S.L., and E. Garcia
  1991   Educating culturally and linguistically diverse preschoolers: Moving the agenda. *Early Childhood Research Quarterly* 6:427-443.
Kirschner Associates, Inc.
  1970   A National Survey of the Impacts of Head Start Centers on Community Institutions. Report prepared for Project Head Start, Office of Child Development, U.S. Department of Health, Education and Welfare, Washington, D.C.

Layzer, J.I., B.D. Goodson, and M. Moss
   1993   *Final Report Volume I: Life in Preschool.* Observational study of early childhood pro-
          grams, prepared for the Office of the Under Secretary, U.S. Department of Education.
          Cambridge, Mass.: Abt Associates.
National Research Council
   1993   *Understanding Child Abuse and Neglect.* Panel on Research on Child Abuse and Neglect.
          Washington, D.C.: National Academy Press.
Osofsky, J.D.
   1995   The effects of exposure to violence on young children. *American Psychologist* 50(9):782-
          788.
Phillips, D., and N. Crowell, eds.
   1994   *Cultural Diversity and Early Education. Report of a Workshop.* Board on Children and
          Families (now Board on Children, Youth, and Families). Washington, D.C.: National
          Academy Press.
Randolph, S.M.
   1995   African American children in single-mother families. Pp. 117-145 in B. Dickerson, ed.,
          African American Single Mothers: Understanding Their Lives and Their Families. Thou-
          sand Oaks, Calif.: Sage Publications, Inc.
Stewart, A.C.
   1994   Head Start Reauthorization Issues and Legislation in the 103rd Congress. Congressional
          Research Service Issue Brief. Library of Congress, Washington, D.C.
Taylor, L., B. Zuckerman, V. Harik, and B. McAlister Groves
   1994   Witnessing violence by young children and their mothers. *Journal of Developmental
          Behavior and Pediatrics* 15:120-123.
U.S. Department of Health and Human Services
   1994   *Head Start Act (As Amended May 18, 1994).* Washington, D.C.: U.S. Department of
          Health and Human Services.
   1993   *Creating A 21st Century Head Start.* Final report of the Advisory Committee on Head
          Start Quality and Expansion. Washington, D.C.: U.S. Department of Health and Human
          Services.
   1990   *Head Start Research and Evaluation: A Blueprint for the Future.* Recommendations of
          the Advisory Panel for the Head Start Evaluation Design Project. Washington, D.C.: U.S.
          Department of Health and Human Services.
U.S. General Accounting Office
   1994   *Early Childhood Programs: Local Perspectives on Barriers to Providing Head Start Ser-
          vices.* Report to the Chairman, Subcommittee on Children, Family, Drugs and Alcohol-
          ism, Committee on Labor and Human Resources, U.S. Senate. Washington, D.C.: U.S.
          General Accounting Office.

A
Excerpts from Two Advisory Committee Reports

This appendix consists of excerpts from two reports by advisory committees of the Administration for Children, Youth, and Families. The first (pp. 58-66) is "Overall Strategy and General Principles" from *Head Start Research and Evaluation: A Blueprint for the Future. Recommendations of the Advisory Panel for the Head Start Evaluation Design Project.* (DHHS publication no. ACY 91-31195, September 1990, Head Start Bureau, Administration for Children, Youth, and Families, Office of Human Development Services, U.S. Department of Health and Human Services).

The second (pp. 60-71) is "Executive Summary" from *Creating a 21st Century Head Start: Final Report of the Advisory Committee on Head Start Quality and Expansion.* (U.S. Government Printing Office 1994—515-032/86864, December 1993, U.S. Department of Health and Human Services, Washington, D.C.).

OVERALL STRATEGY AND GENERAL PRINCIPLES

Future Head Start research and evaluation efforts should be guided by a clearly defined overall strategy and general principles. This section presents and discusses the eight principles formulated by the Panel.

1. Head Start research and evaluation planning should be organized around two principal questions:

- **Which Head Start practices maximize benefits for children and families with different characteristics under what types of circumstances?**

- **How are gains sustained for children and families after the Head Start experience?**

Research initiatives designed to answer these questions offer high promise of producing information that will lead to continuing improvements in the quality of Head Start and other early childhood programs. Moreover, careful consideration of these pivotal questions will help ACYF identify Head Start factors and post-Head Start experiences that extend or attenuate the positive effects of the Head Start program.

The nature of these two principal questions defines a new generation of research and evaluation which differs significantly from past studies. First, they require much finer grained analyses, particularly with respect to independent variables. Second, they require information specific to various subgroups of the Head Start population. Third, they recognize the contribution of the knowledge of context to the interpretation of data. Fourth, they acknowledge family functioning, both as a goal in itself and its importance in the mediation of the child's development. Each of these research and evaluation implications will be discussed further in this report.

2. An overall research strategy rather than a single large scale study is the appropriate framework for addressing critical Head Start research and evaluation questions.

The Panel recommends strongly against a single large scale study of Head Start as the principal mechanism for seeking answers to the pivotal research questions highlighted above. The methodological requirements for the new generation of research and evaluation issues do not lend themselves to large scale evaluations that treat Head Start as a single program. Head Start is not, in any simple sense, a uniform "treatment." The common denominator of Head Start programs nationwide is conformity to a set of regulatory performance standards that reflect comprehensive service requirements in education, parent involvement, social services, and health services. But programs are allowed and encouraged broad flexibility in how they deliver the required component services. Moreover, Head Start programs serve children in different regions and subeconomies of American society. They serve a number of minority groups and address issues of bilingualism and multiculturalism. They embody a variety of programmatic formulas and inventions created by local Head Start staff to respond to the unique needs of families in their communities.

An overall strategy is needed to extend existing theory and state-of-the-art research methods and to provide a more comprehensive and in-depth knowledge base for improving the quality of services provided to children and families. The Panel proposes three key approaches to guide this new strategy. These are implementation of an integrated set of studies, use of diverse methodologies and identification of marker variables.

Implementation of an Integrated and Coordinated Set of Research and Evaluation Studies Collectively Designed to Address the Major Questions.

An advantage of multiple studies, as opposed to a single large project, is the capacity for a cluster of studies to complement one another at a single point in time and to build upon one another in incremental stages over time. A further advantage is the ability to cross-validate findings using different methodologies and to test the hypotheses with different subgroups of programs and participants.

The research and evaluation studies should be designed to yield results that are interpretable for specific subgroups of children and/or families and for specific localities. These findings, taken as a whole, could address the major questions of interest. In addition, the studies should be designed and conducted by a consortium of investigators who would contribute a number of different perspectives and areas of expertise to the effort. Such an arrangement permits much more control over the quality of the data than is possible in large scale studies that are under the direction of an individual investigator or contracting firm.

The necessity for an integrated and coordinated set of studies cannot be overemphasized. Although a large number of studies of Head Start were conducted over the past 25 years (particularly in the first dozen years of the program's existence), what exists is a fractionated accumulation of studies that do not build upon one another. These efforts have yielded relatively little in the way of an organized body of knowledge. Head Start research and evaluation, in general, has not been based upon well formulated program and policy questions.

Use of Diverse Methodologies

The need for different research designs depends on the state of knowledge and the particular issues being explored. The proposed strategy draws upon diverse methodologies including case, ethnographic, correlational, quasi-experimental, and experimental studies. The common denominator of these various designs should be an overall conceptual framework guided by the principal questions.

Correlational and quasi-experimental studies could be used to test hypothetical causal models, models of "What works best for whom?" and of factors conducive to the maintenance of gains. Such studies could also identify variables that suggest causal influences or "active ingredients." Experiments could be designed to test these hypotheses through treatment manipulations or modifications, or additions to existing Head Start programs in randomized trials. This is one example of how a particular issue could be pursued through several stages of inquiry. There are many variations on this theme depending on the particular questions to be explored and the available research and evaluation resources.

It is important to note that, in the view of the Panel, randomized studies designed to compare the effects of Head Start against the effects of nonparticipation ("treatment vs. no treatment") are generally no longer viable options. First, as ACYF progresses toward the

Administration's goal of universal services for all eligible children, the potential for withholding services to form a control group, already difficult for ethical and practical reasons, will cease to be an option. Second, in view of the expansion of state and public school preschool programs and developmental child care, it is unrealistic to expect to find in most communities a representative group of "untreated" eligible children, even if Head Start services are not provided.

There are a variety of ways to respond to these and other constraints on experimental options posed by changing societal realities. One approach would be to use random assignment at the level of individual Head Start programs, centers, classrooms, or groups of home visitors to test various experimental "add ons." The control comparison would be an individual Head Start program (or unit or units) from the same subpopulation that did not receive the "add ons."

Case and ethnographic studies have played an increasingly important role in social science methodology. First, they are particularly helpful for hypothesis formulation. Second, knowledge of how programs actually operate, why something works or does not work, why some strategies work for children and families with a particular set of characteristics and not for others and the conditions under which they work are best informed by qualitative methodologies. Quantitative research does not replace qualitative knowledge, but instead builds upon it and requires it for valid interpretation. Both quantitative and qualitative research must conform to appropriate scientific criteria for assembling and analyzing evidence in order to insure the validity, reliability, and replicability of the findings.

In the past, one of the detriments to the use of qualitative methods has been the high cost of the methodology. However, if high quality research is to be conducted to respond to the critical issues in Head Start, then future Head Start studies must use both qualitative and quantitative methods in a complementary fashion.

Identification of Marker Variables

Another necessary condition for an integrated and coordinated set of studies is the identification of a set of *marker variables* for child functioning, family functioning, program characteristics, and community characteristics. These core variables will make it possible to tie separate studies together. Identification of marker variables should take place early in the implementation of the next series of Head Start studies, either as an integral part of the initial studies or as a separate activity. Additional variables would be added to particular studies, depending on the specific questions under investigation. Marker variables should be sensitive to racial, ethnic, linguistic, and cultural diversity among Head Start subpopulations.

In summary, the Panel recommends a strategy that involves an integrated set of small scale studies involving different methodologies, different subgroups of the Head Start population and multiple investigators. However, use of small scale studies does not mean that findings and policy decisions will be based on small samples. Nor does this mean that these studies would be simple in design. Rather, the recommended strategy will facilitate the convergence of results from multiple sources that will collectively incorporate robust findings from sophisticated designs. Thus the study outcomes will say something meaningful about the impact on subgroups of program participants.

3. **The diversity of Head Start children and families as well as the diversity of the communities in which they reside must be recognized explicitly in future evaluation and research.**

Head Start families and children are not all alike. The problems faced by an African-American child growing up in an inner city neighborhood are only broadly like those of a Native American child on an Indian reservation, a child growing up in a depressed area of Appalachia, or a Spanish-speaking child in the migrant stream. It is essential that future research and evaluation on the efficacy of Head Start address the program effects for these diverse populations.

Specific populations can be defined by such factors as presence and type of child disabilities, children's health status (including lingering effects of parental substance abuse), family composition and functioning, racial and ethnic status, linguistic differences, geographic area of residence, and other variables (or combinations of variables) that encompass the wide diversity of such subgroups.

The community attributes that may be relevant to program and policy development include the characteristics of neighborhoods in which the children reside (for example, inner city, rural, suburban, or migrant; areas of concentrated poverty and social dislocation; areas with minimal health, education, and social services; and degree of homogeneity/heterogeneity in the population).

Previous research on early childhood programs has to some degree taken subpopulations into account by further subdivision of their original sample at the time of analysis. However, the important subpopulation issues have not been addressed. Subpopulation issues must be considered and incorporated into the initial design of all future studies.

The fundamental reason for considering subgroup populations from the outset of research planning is the likelihood that modifications in site selection, in the selection of independent and dependent variables, and in instrumentation may prove necessary to take into account specific subgroups. If a proper foundation is not laid at the research design phase, it will be difficult, and sometimes impossible, to rectify the situation during analysis.

For example, readiness to learn is a reasonable objective for Head Start children. To attain Head Start's goal of social competence, program staff must facilitate the child's learning in developmentally appropriate ways and enhance future prospects for success in formal schooling. However, this objective may need to be redefined, sometimes radically, for children with certain disabling conditions or for children whose dominant language is other than English. Each subgroup with disabilities or with language differences can benefit from participation in Head Start. However, the expected outcomes (dependent variables) may differ, with implications for measurement selection and data collection techniques. Such subgroup considerations are particularly salient in addressing the question "What works best for whom?"

4. **Evaluation research must explicitly address diverse outcome indices related to children, families, communities and institutions.**

Historically, Head Start has embraced multiple goals affecting children, families, and other institutions and conditions within the local community. Yet in the past, studies of Head Start have overwhelmingly focused on child outcomes, particularly outcomes in the cognitive and language domains. Little attention has been given to child outcomes in the domains of socioemotional and physical development. Even less emphasis has been devoted to the impact on families, other institutions, and the community ecology.

Child outcomes should remain a central thrust of Head Start studies. However, the focus of future Head Start research and evaluation efforts should be widened to include a broader array of child outcomes and to encompass outcomes for families, communities, and institutions.

Head Start is a *two generation program* that, in addition to the social competence goals for children, addresses goals for parents and other family members as priority outcomes in their own right. For example, Head Start's initiatives in the areas of family literacy, job training, and family support incorporate objectives of parental educational attainment, employability, and family self-sufficiency. ACYF's research agenda should give high priority to issues of family functioning, parent involvement in their children's development, family support, and family variables as mediating influences on child functioning.

Examples of salient family outcomes of a Head Start experience include:

- improved parenting skills;

- increased parent-child interaction to promote child development and learning and to strengthen the family system;

- improved expectations for children's future success in school;

- increased parent involvement in schools and other community institutions;

- reduced risk factors associated with family stress, including family violence, child abuse and neglect and substance abuse;

- reduced dependence on welfare and heightened parental skills related to economic self-sufficiency (for example, improved literacy, adult education, and employability); and

- improved access to and utilization of community family support services.

In pursuit of its multiple program goals, Head Start has forged new relationships with agencies at the Federal, state and local levels and served as a catalyst in developing partnerships among human services agencies. The nature of such collaboration is an area of inquiry in terms of the impact of Head Start's efforts on policy and on the delivery of social programs and must be taken into account in research design and in the selection of independent variables.

5. Multiple indicators and methods should be employed in the measurement of important outcomes.

Evaluations should utilize, to the fullest extent possible, outcome indicators that are reflective of the generally understood goals of Head Start and that convey the program's important effects. These outcome measures should be readily understandable to parents, program staff, policymakers, and the general public. In addition to carefully selected standardized tests, outcome measures should include such straightforward indicators as whether or not a child is at grade level, is placed in a special class, or does or does not have an undetected (or identified but untreated) medical condition.

Researchers should be mindful, however, that there are often complex dimensions of "simple" measures of the type recommended. For example, whether a child is retained in grade in the public schools is a relatively simple indicator. Why the child is retained in grade, the criteria by which this decision is made, and the implications for the child's future success in school may vary greatly within and across different school systems. Similarly, whether or not a child is in a special education class or experiencing "pull out" instruction is relatively easy to establish. What this means in terms of the child's placement in an appropriate educational environment that will best meet the child's learning and developmental needs is more complex.

In general, previous Head Start studies used norm-referenced tests either of I.Q. or achievement as the single method for measuring program outcomes. There has been well justified criticism of the use of I.Q. tests, particularly for minority children. However, there are other norm-referenced tests that are useful in determining the child's acquisition of certain skills. In fact, familiarity with "taking tests" and the particular skills involved in the test process can serve the child well in terms of future academic demands.

Norm-referenced tests should be only one of several methods for measuring child status. Indicators of a child's status, such as reading ability, number competence, or ability to function as a confident social participant in classroom and school processes are best arrived at through multiple methods, including observations, and ratings by teachers, parents, and peers.

Care should be taken in the selection of child outcome instruments to keep in mind that the ultimate purpose is to assess program effectiveness. With respect to school readiness and achievement, for example, the focus should be on the extent to which the influences of Head Start, school and the family combine to provide the child with opportunities to learn and function in an educational setting at an optimal level consistent with his or her ability.

The overall Head Start evaluation agenda should strive to balance the following elements: validity of outcome measures, ease of data collection for both researchers and program staff, multimethod assessment strategies, and an understanding of the underlying dynamics that the indicators purport to represent.

6. Data collection procedures and techniques must be valid and appropriate for the particular research question and the specific population.

Any norm-referenced instruments used with particular subpopulations must be valid for the subpopulation under consideration. Interviews and questionnaires administered to parents must take into account literacy level and linguistic usage of the respondents. In order to insure reliability and validity of the responses, these instruments may require special adaptations for different subpopulations. Of particular importance is attention to predictive validity. Reliable instruments may differ substantially in their capacity to predict the same outcome for different subpopulations. Therefore, most instruments will, of necessity, have to be pilot-tested prior to their use in research and evaluation studies.

All instruments should be administered individually to Head Start children. To optimize measurement comparability across years, individually administered tests also should be employed in later grade school followups.

7. Program variation must be explored while searching for explanations of differential outcomes.

There is no single active ingredient in Head Start that is the key to program outcomes. Local Head Start programs are complex organizational entities that interact with equally complex family and community ecologies. This calls for a combination of holistic research strategies (including organizational, case study, and ethnographic methodologies) together with multivariate statistical explorations involving natural variation, experimental, and quasi-experimental designs. Researchers should be alert to the possibilities that interaction of program attributes may be more important in accounting for outcomes than individual program attributes considered in isolation.

The following program variables are among those that are particularly important:

- staff characteristics and behaviors (including education, years of experience, credentials and certification, length and type of training, and knowledge of early childhood education and child development);

- classroom composition (group size and child-staff ratio) and, for home-based programs, family-home visitor case loads;

- nature and intensity of interactions among children and between children and staff;

- curricular strategy, including the extent to which the curriculum is well-planned and appropriately delivered;

- nature and intensity of parent involvement;

- staff-parent interaction;

- nature and frequency of home visiting and other family contacts;

- delivery of comprehensive services, including nature of linkages with health, nutrition, social and educational agencies;

- length and intensity of child's participation per day, week, and year;

- age at onset of intervention and number of years of child's and family's participation in the program;

- degree of program responsiveness to identified needs of participating children and families;

- extent and nature of flexibility exercised by the local program in tailoring its delivery system to specific circumstances and resources in the community;

- organizational climate;

- administrative and personnel issues (including staff compensation and turnover); and

- program auspices.

Head Start research should capitalize on the insights of prior and ongoing research in early childhood education, child development, and other related fields in exploring these variables. For example, organizational research is currently bringing new understandings to the functioning of public schools. Similar perspectives on examining Head Start programs as organizational entities can provide powerful research tools. Areas of inquiry include leadership, how decisions are made, the role of parent participation on policy councils, grantee-delegate agency linkages, the relationships of local programs and ACYF Regional Offices, and approaches to program implementation. Related administrative and personnel issues are worthy of priority attention, as suggested by recent findings in child care research showing the strong relationship between staff salaries and turnover and child outcomes.

In addition to variation across programs, variation within programs must be explored. Children and families vary considerably in the attributes with which they enter Head Start programs. These attributes will differ in their interactions with program characteristics. Therefore, even families with children in the same classrooms will vary in their Head Start experiences. Traditional methodology assumes a uniform treatment across families, at least among those with children in the same classroom. In studies which explore the reasons for differential effects, it is crucial to incorporate consideration of such variation in the initial design of the study.

8. Head Start research and evaluation studies can be greatly enhanced by building on the existing strengths of programs and program staffs.

The Panel felt strongly that researchers need to approach all studies with a focus on identifying the strengths of current programs and program staffs, rather than emphasizing deficits (for similar reasons that the approach to children and families should emphasize strengths rather than deficits). Research projects are most likely to succeed if researchers include program staff in all stages of the project, including the initial development of hypotheses. Collaboration between the research and program communities calls for joint planning with clearly defined roles and benefits for all parties.

Studies of existing programs are most likely to bear fruit if they involve a search for excellence both in overall programs and in particular strengths within programs. In addition, experimental designs to test program features will be most successful if those program "add ons" are considered by Head Start staff as new and exciting additions to their current programs. It also is important to provide increased funding to offset the costs of implementing the added features.

Although cooperative efforts between program and evaluation staff are essential, data collection procedures must include safeguards to insure that findings are not subject to the criticism of respondent bias. Such safeguards might include the use of ratings by independent observers not connected with a program. In addition, program staff should receive guarantees that negative findings will not be used by administrators to penalize the program or eliminate its staff. These guarantees are likely to reduce respondent bias and enhance the quality of the data.

Budgetary Considerations

The Panel's chief concern is that high quality research is conducted and used to make future decisions about programs that can profoundly affect the lives of poor children and their families. In addition to the recommended principles that undergird the research strategy discussed above, the following corollary principles involve budgetary considerations.

- High quality research is expensive. A smaller number of adequately funded studies is preferred to a larger number of inadequately funded efforts.

- The first year of all large scale and complex studies should be devoted to design and pilot testing. For all studies, there should be sufficient lead time prior to the formal data collection stage to permit careful pilot testing and the refining and fine-tuning of the design, measurement instruments and procedures.

Executive Summary

The Advisory Committee on Head Start Quality and Expansion was created in June 1993 to review the Head Start program and make recommendations for improvement and expansion. After six months of deliberations, the 47 members of the Advisory Committee seek to open a new chapter in the history of the program.

Launched in 1965 as a comprehensive child development program, Head Start has provided a beacon of hope and support to more than 13 million low-income children and their families across the United States through the provision of education, health, social services, parent involvement, and disability services.

Yet the world of Head Start today is dramatically different than in 1965. Today the needs of families and children who live in poverty are more complicated and urgent than ever before—from children who have lived with violence and substance abuse to families with interrelated problems of homelessness, lack of education, and unemployment. Since Head Start began, the face of poverty has changed to include more single parents, and increasing numbers of working parents. In addition, the recognition and importance of promoting family literacy has increased.

Over the past 28 years, the landscape of community services has changed dramatically. There are new roles and enhanced capacities for serving young children and their families. Today we also have new knowledge about the attributes of services and supports that are effective in changing long-term outcomes for young children, new knowledge about the importance of the first three years of life, and new knowledge and appreciation for the continuum of developmental and comprehensive services needed before school and into the early years to help children succeed in school.

In order to develop a set of recommendations for the future of the Head Start program, the Advisory Committee reviewed existing data and reports on Head Start and consulted with a wide variety of individuals and groups across the country. The Committee found that, after a period of rapid expansion, Head Start can be proud of many successes yet still needs to address existing quality problems and to be refocused to meet the challenges of a new age. The Advisory Committee found that:

The Report of the Advisory Committee on Head Start Quality and Expansion

---

☐ Head Start has been successful in improving the lives of many low-income children and their families and in serving as a national laboratory for early childhood and family support;

☐ Most Head Start programs provide quality services, however, the quality of programs is uneven across the country;

☐ Head Start needs to be better equipped to serve the diverse needs of families;

☐ There continues to be a large unmet need for Head Start services; and

☐ In many communities and states, Head Start, public schools, and other early childhood programs and providers responsible for addressing the needs of young children and families operate in isolation from one another, without adequate resources, planning, and coordination.

As the Advisory Committee looks forward to the next century, we envision an expanded and renewed Head Start which serves as a central community institution for low-income children and their families. The Head Start of the 21st century:

☐ Ensures quality and strives to attain excellence in every local program;

☐ Responds flexibly to the needs of today's children and families, including those currently unserved; and

☐ Forges new partnerships at the community, state, and federal levels, renewing and recrafting these partnerships to fit the changes in families, communities, and state and national policy.

In order to respond to these issues, and to create a 21st Century Head Start, the Advisory Committee sets forth a set of recommendations to the federal government, Head Start providers, and the nation at large. These recommendations implement three broad principles.

*1. We must ensure that every Head Start program can deliver on Head Start's vision, by striving for **excellence** in serving both children and families.*

The Advisory Committee believes that the quality of services must be a first priority. We should strive for excellence in all Head Start programs by focusing on staffing and career development, improving the management of local programs, reengineering federal oversight to assure accountability, providing better facilities, and strengthening the role of research.

The Advisory Committee recommends that the Department of Health and Human Services (HHS) develop new initiatives to utilize qualified "mentor teachers" to provide supervision and support to classroom staff, establish competency-based training for staff who work directly with families, ensure sufficient staffing levels to serve children and families effectively, and continue to increase compensation.

In the area of management, the Advisory Committee recommends an expanded emphasis on management training; strengthening financial management policies and practices; supporting strategic planning through a multi-year "phased-in" expansion strategy; updating the Performance Standards in health, parent involvement, social services, and education; and developing performance measures.

In addition, the Advisory Committee recommends an assessment of the training and technical assistance system, a review and strengthening of Head Start monitoring, training of regional and central office staff, and the assurance of prompt action to deal with low performing grantees.

2. We must expand the number of children served and the scope of services provided in a way that is more responsive to the needs of ***children and families.***

The Advisory Committee reaffirms the concept that all eligible children in need of Head Start should be served. At the same time the Committee remains committed to investments in quality as a top priority. Head Start should focus on the needs of children in the context of their families and communities by enhancing family services and increasing parent involvement, assessing needs and planning strategically, reaching out to children and families currently unserved, promoting full day and full year programs where needed, and improving services to families with younger children. The overwhelming majority of Advisory Committee members recommend a new initiative to expand Head Start services to families with younger children. Some Advisory Committee members believe that further study is needed to explore ways of serving additional families with children under age three prior to launching an initiative.

The Advisory Committee recommends that HHS review and expand current resources used for family services, parent education, and family literacy, and that increased efforts be made to involve parents in all aspects of the program. The Committee recommends that as Head Start programs move forward toward the goal of serving all eligible children, they should be encouraged to assess their total program in order to balance the needs for quality, scope of services, and number of children served. Particular attention and support are recommended to address the special needs of Indian and migrant programs.

*3. We must encourage Head Start to forge **partnerships** with key community and state institutions and programs in early childhood, family support, health, education, and mental health, and we must ensure that these partnerships are constantly renewed and recrafted to fit changes in families, communities, and state and national policies.*

Because no program, no matter how excellent, can go it alone, we must ensure that Head Start join forces with other providers in the community and state. As a partner, Head Start can not only maximize its own resources, but can use its leadership to influence other service providers to adopt the core concepts that have made Head Start such a success.

Head Start and public schools should renew commitments to ensure continuity of services by providing developmentally appropriate programs, parent involvement, and supportive services from Head Start through the primary grades.

Head Start should form new partnerships at the state and local level, and with the private sector, to provide more coordinated services to families. Head Start should also play a central role on behalf of low-income children and families in emerging initiatives, particularly in national service, health reform, education reform, family preservation and support and welfare reform.

In summary, the Advisory Committee supports the goal of ensuring that all eligible children and their families receive high quality Head Start services, that programs are tailored to meet the needs of todays families and communities, and that sufficient resources are made available to meet these goals.

The Advisory Committee believes that the recommendations and principles set forth in this report must inform Head Start program decisions at all levels. The recommendations must guide priorities and the use of existing as well as new resources to ensure quality services that children need to enter school ready to learn and that families need to achieve self-sufficiency.

The Advisory Committee recommends that HHS act promptly to develop an implementation plan based on the ideas set forth in this report. First priority should be given to ensuring quality and striving for excellence.

The process of setting priorities should also draw on the best available information and input from Head Start and the larger community.

In concluding, the Advisory Committee on Head Start Quality and Expansion urges the Department to see this report as a step in an overall effort to improve early childhood and family support services for all children in the United States, and particularly for those most vulnerable. HHS should continue to show leadership in looking across programs to ensure that policies consistently promote quality services for young children and their families.

Workshop Agendas and Speakers

DEMOGRAPHICS, LIFE CIRCUMSTANCES, AND NEEDS OF
HEAD START AND HEAD START-ELIGIBLE FAMILIES

November 21-22, 1994
Georgetown University Conference Center
3800 Reservoir Road, NW
Washington, DC

Chair, Sheldon White

NOVEMBER 21, 1994

8:30 - 9:00   **Continental Breakfast**

9:00 - 9:15   **Welcome and Opening Remarks**
                Speaker: *Sheldon White*, Harvard University

9:15 - 10:00   **Overview of Head Start: Contemporary Context for
                Policy and Research and Charge to the Roundtable**
                Speakers: **Olivia Golden** and **Helen Taylor**
                Administration on Children, Youth, and Families,
                U.S. Department of Health and Human Services

10:00 - 10:45   **Demographics of Head Start Families**
                Roundtable Member: **Gregg Powell**, National Head
                Start Association
                Speaker: **Sandra Hofferth**, University of Michigan

10:45 - 11:00   **Break**

11:00 - 11:45   **Teenage Parents/Multigenerational Families**
Roundtable Member and Speaker: **Suzanne Randolph,**
University of Maryland

11:45 - 12:30   **Community Context: Children and Violence**
Roundtable Member: **Claudia Coulton,** Case Western
Reserve University
Speaker: **Barry Zuckerman,** Boston City Hospital

12:30 - 1:30   **Lunch**

1:30 - 2:15   **Mental Health Needs of Head Start Children and
Families**
Roundtable Member and Speaker: **Jane Knitzer,**
National Center for Children in Poverty

2:15 - 3:00   **Needs of Language-Minority Families**
Roundtable Member: **Eugene Garcia,** U.S. Department
of Education
Speaker: **Luis Laosa,** Education Testing Service

3:00 - 3:15   **Break**

3:15 - 4:00   **Needs of AFDC/JOBS Mothers**
Roundtable Member: **Martha Moorehouse,** Office of the
Assistant Secretary for Planning and Evaluation,
U.S. Department of Health and Human Services
Speaker: **Randale Valenti,** Department of Public Aid,
Illinois

CLOSED SESSION

4:00 - 5:15   **Bias Discussion for Roundtable Members**

5:15 - 6:00   **Reception with Invited Guests and Speakers**

6:00 - 8:00   **Dinner: Roundtable Members and Invited Speakers**

NOVEMBER 22, 1994

8:30 - 9:00   **Continental Breakfast**

9:00 - 9:45   **Experiences of Migrant Families**
Roundtable Member: Carole Clarke, Center for
Education and Manpower Resources
Speaker: **Mary Lou de Leon Siantz**, Indiana University

CLOSED SESSION

9:45 - 11:00   **Discussion of Issues Raised in the Presentations**

11:00 - 11:15   **Break**

11:15 - 12:30   **Continued Discussion of Issues Raised in Presentations**

12:30 - 1:30   **Lunch**

1:30 - 2:00   **Plans for Next Meetings**

EFFECTS AND EXPERIENCES
OF FAMILY-LEVEL INTERVENTIONS

December 16-17, 1994
National Research Council
2001 Wisconsin Avenue, NW
Washington, DC

Chair, Sheldon White

DECEMBER 16, 1994

8:30 - 9:00   Continental Breakfast

9:00 - 9:15   **Welcome and Opening Remarks**
               Speaker: **Sheldon White**, Harvard University

9:15 - 9:45   **Charge to the Roundtable**
               Speaker: **Olivia Golden**, Administration on Children,
               Youth, and Families, U.S. Department of Health and
               Human Services

9:45 - 10:45   **Frameworks for Examining the Effects of Family
               Support Initiatives**

               Head Start in the Context of Family Support Models
               Roundtable Member: **Heather Weiss**, Harvard Graduate
               School of Education

               Issues in Designing a Family Support Program
               Evaluation
               Speakers: **Jean Layzer**, Abt Associates, and
               Lynn Kagan, Bush Center on Child Development
               and Social Policy, Yale University

10:45 - 11:00 **Break**

11:00 - 12:30   **Supporting Parent Involvement**
Roundtable Member: **Willie Epps,** Southern Illinois
University, Edwardsville

Current Vision and Strategy for Involving Parents in
Head Start
Speaker: **Marlys Gustafson,** Administration on
Children, Youth, and Families, U.S. Department of
Health and Human Services

Intervention Strategies for Hard-to-Engage Parents
Speaker: **Susan Young,** Staten Island Mental Health
Society

Reaching Fathers
Speaker: **James Levine,** Families and Work Institute

12:30 - 1:30   **Lunch**

1:30 - 3:00   **Supporting Family Self-Sufficiency: Head Start and
Other Programs**
Roundtable Member: **Valora Washington,** W.K. Kellogg
Foundation

Head Start Family Service Centers
Speaker: **Janet Swartz,** Abt Associates

Comprehensive Child Development Centers
Speaker: **Robert St. Pierre,** Abt Associates, and
Michael Lopez, Administration on Children, Youth,
and Families, U.S. Department of Health and Human
Services

Project Match: Step-Up With Head Start
Speaker: **Toby Herr,** Project Match

3:00 - 3:15   **Break**

3:15 - 4:45   **Addressing Health and Mental Health Needs**
                   Roundtable Member: **Jack Shonkoff**, Brandeis
                   University

                   Effects of Managed-Care on the Health Needs of Poor
                   Families
                   Speaker: **Sara Rosenbaum**, George Washington
                   University

                   Mental Health Consultation: Serving Caregivers and
                   Families
                   Speaker: **Kadija Johnston**, University of California,
                   San Francisco

                   Free to Grow Project: A Community Perspective
                   Speaker: **John Love**, Mathematica Policy Research Inc.

4:45 - 5:30   **Summing Up: Issues for Research**
                   Speakers: **Heather Weiss**, Harvard Graduate School of
                   Education, **Jean Layzer**, Abt Associates, and
                   Lynn Kagan, Bush Center on Child Development and
                   Social Policy, Yale University

5:30 - 6:00   **Reception with Invited Guests and Speakers**

6:00 - 8:00   **Dinner: Roundtable Members and Invited Speakers**

DECEMBER 17, 1994

8:00 - 8:30   **Continental Breakfast**

8:30 - 10:15   **Discussion of Issues Raised in the Presentations**

10:15 - 10:30   **Break**

10:30 - 12:00   **Continued Discussion of Issues**

12:00 - 1:00   **Lunch with Speaker**
Caring for Young Children in Violent Environments
Speaker: **Joy Osofsky**, Louisiana State University

1:00 - 2:00   **Closing Discussion**

DIVERSITY AND IMPLICATIONS FOR HEAD START

January 12-13, 1995
National Research Council
2001 Wisconsin Avenue, NW
Washington, DC

Chair, Sheldon White

JANUARY 12, 1995

8:30 - 9:00   **Continental Breakfast**

9:00 - 9:15   **Welcome and Opening Remarks**
                 Speaker: Sheldon White, Harvard University

9:15 - 10:15   **Alternative Family Structure Among Poor Families:
                 Issues for Head Start**
                 Speaker: **Robin Jarret,** Loyola University of Chicago

10:15 - 10:30   **Break**

10:30 - 11:30   **Challenges of Serving Immigrant Families and
                 Children**
                 Speaker: **Deborah Phillips,** Board on Children, Youth,
                 and Families

11:30 - 12:30   **Meeting the Needs of Language-Minority Children
                 in Head Start**
                 Speaker: **Claude Goldenberg**, California State
                 University, Long Beach

12:30 - 1:30   **Lunch**

1:30 - 2:00   **Discussion of Working Group Assignments**

2:00 - 4:00   **Working Group Meetings**

4:15 - 5:30	Reports From Working Groups and Discussion
5:30 - 6:00	Reception with Invited Guests and Speakers
6:00 - 8:00	Dinner with Roundtable Members and Invited Speakers

JANUARY 13, 1995

8:30 - 9:00	Continental Breakfast
9:00 - 10:00	Continuation of Bias Discussions
10:00 - 12:00	Continuation of Working Groups
12:00 - 1:00	Lunch
1:00 - 2:00	Final Summing Up

WORKSHOP SPEAKERS

John Busa, Administration on Children, Youth, and Families, Washington, DC

Carole Clarke, Center for Education and Manpower Resource, Ukiah, CA

Mary Lou de Leon Siantz, Indiana University

Olivia Golden, Administration on Children, Youth, and Families, Washington, DC

Claude Goldenberg, California State University, Long Beach, CA

Jim Griffin, Administration on Children, Youth, and Families, Washington, DC

Marlys Gustafson, Administration on Children, Youth, and Families, Washington, DC

Toby Herr, Project Match, Erikson Institute, Chicago, IL

Sandra Hofferth, Institute for Social Research, University of Michigan

Robin Jarret, Loyola University of Chicago

Kadija Johnston, University of California, San Francisco

Sharon Lynn Kagan, Bush Center on Child Develpment and Social Policy, Yale University

Jane Knitzer, National Center for Children in Poverty, New York, NY

Luis Laosa, Education Testing Service, Princeton, NJ

Jean Layzer, Abt Associates, New York, NY

James Levine, Families and Work Institute, New York, NY

Michael Lopez, Administration on Children, Youth, and Families, Washington, DC

John Love, Mathematica Policy Research, Inc., Princeton, NJ

Ruth Hubel McKey, Administration on Children, Youth, and Families, Washington, DC

Joy Osofsky, Lousiana State University

Deborah Phillips, Board on Children, Youth, and Families

Gregg Powell, National Head Start Association, Alexandria, VA

Suzanne Randolph, University of Maryland

Sara Rosenbaum, George Washington University

Robert St. Pierre, Abt Associates, New York, NY

Janet Swartz, Abt Associates, Cambridge, MA

Helen Taylor, Administration on Children, Youth, and Families, Washington, DC

Randale Valenti, Department of Public Aid, Springfield, IL
Heather Weiss, Graduate School of Education, Harvard University
Susan Young, Staten Island Mental Health Society, Staten Island, NY
Barry Zuckerman, Boston City Hospital, Boston, MA

Other Reports from the Board on Children, Youth, and Families

Child Care for Low-Income Families: Directions for Research. Summary of a Workshop (1996)

Service Provider Perspectives on Family Violence Interventions: Proceedings of a Workshop (1995)

"Immigrant Children and Their Families: Issues for Research and Policy" in *The Future of Children* (1995)

Integrating Federal Statistics on Children: Report of a Workshop (with the Committee on National Statistics of the National Research Council) (1995)

Child Care for Low-Income Families: Report of Two Workshops (1995)

New Findings on Children, Families, and Economic Self-Sufficiency: Summary of a Research Briefing (1995)

Cultural Diversity and Early Education: Report of a Workshop (1994)

Benefits and Systems of Care for Maternal and Child Health: Workshop Highlights (with the Board on Health Promotion and Disease Prevention of the Institute of Medicine) (1994)

Protecting and Improving the Quality of Children Under Health Care Reform: Workshop Highlights (with the Board on Health Promotion and Disease Prevention of the Institute of Medicine) (1994)

America's Fathers and Public Policy: Report of a Workshop (1994)